The ROCK, *the* ROAD, *and the* RABBI

Come to the Land Where It All Began

BIBLE STUDY GUIDE | SIX SESSIONS

KATHIE LEE GIFFORD
WITH RABBI JASON SOBEL

STUDY GUIDE BY KAREN LEE-THORP

HarperChristian Resources

The Rock, the Road, and the Rabbi Bible Study Guide
© 2018, 2023 by Kathie Lee Gifford

Published in Grand Rapids, Michigan, by HarperChristian Resources. HarperChristian Resources is a registered trademark of HarperCollins Christian Publishing, Inc.

Requests for information should be sent to customercare@harpercollins.com.

ISBN 978-0-310-14717-6 (softcover)
ISBN 978-0-310-14718-3 (ebook)

HarperChristian Resources titles may be purchased in bulk for church, business, fundraising, or ministry use. For information, please e-mail ResourceSpecialist@ChurchSource.com.

First Printing April 2018 / Printed in the United States of America

CONTENTS

How to Use This Guide

The land that God promised to Abraham and his descendants is a dry, rocky piece of dirt roughly the size of New Hampshire. It has been quarreled over for millennia because it lies on a land bridge linking Asia and Africa and is thus a key part of the trade route between those two continents. Every time an empire from the Middle East wanted to expand into North Africa (or vice versa), its army had to march through what we call the Holy Land.

Some of the events of the Bible took place outside the Holy Land, but the whole of Jesus' earthly life was spent there. So, if we want to understand what His life was about, we are well served to know about the places where He lived and taught and died and rose again. This study aims to bring those places alive in ways that will illuminate the message of the Gospels, the message of Jesus. You will also be discovering the very Jewish background of the Gospels in ways that sheds fresh light on the Scriptures. If you think you already know what happened in Bethlehem or Jerusalem, get ready to be amazed!

Before you begin, keep in mind there are a few ways you can go through this material. You can experience this study with others in a group (such as a Bible study or small-group gathering), or you may choose to go through the content on your own. Either way, know that the videos for each session are available for you to view at any time via streaming.

This guide contains six sessions that accompany the video teachings. You can meet weekly for six weeks or proceed at a slower pace. Each session contains these sections:

- **Today's Tour Stop:** An introduction to the places that you will be exploring.
- **First Thoughts:** A few icebreaker-type questions that will help you get to know others in your group as you start discussing the session's theme. After session one, you will also have a chance to share insights you gained from doing the Digging Deeper work between sessions.
- **Watch the Video:** Includes an outline of key thoughts from the video segment, along with space to write your own notes of what stands out to you.
- **Debriefing the Tour (Group Discussion):** Questions for your group to discuss. You'll interact with the Bible, the video, and your own stories.
- **Trying It Out:** A fun and enlightening exercise that lets you do something with what you're learning other than just talking about it.

- **That's a Wrap:** A summary of the teachings in the session.
- **Closing Prayer:** An idea for how to guide your group prayer time as you finish your meeting.
- **Recommended Reading:** The chapters in *The Rock, the Road, and the Rabbi* book that correspond to each week's study.
- **Digging Deeper:** Questions for you to investigate on your own before the next session. Ideally, you'll want to do these exercises over several sittings rather than trying to do all of them at one time. The exercises are divided into three days, but you can spread them out over more days if you prefer.

For group meetings, you will need a copy of this study guide, a Bible, a pen, and an open heart. For the solo work between meetings, you will need:

- A copy of Kathie Lee Gifford's and Rabbi Jason Sobel's book *The Rock, the Road, and the Rabbi*
- A Bible
- A pen
- Extra paper or a journal, in case you need more room to express your thoughts

If you're going to do the "Trying It Out" section of each session, your group leader will need to plan ahead and bring some materials. The materials for each session are:

Session 1: Cardboard, felt tip pens, white ribbon, and tape
Session 2: Paper and pens
Session 3: Paper and felt tip pens or pencils
Session 4: No materials
Session 5: Palm branches or stones the size of paper weights, and magic markers
Session 6: Laptop, tablet, or smartphone for internet search

FOR GROUP LEADERS

Everything you need to lead your group is right here in this study guide. In each session, watch for the instructions in italics immediately under each section heading. If your group is newly formed, you may find it helpful to go over a few simple ground rules in your first meeting. These can help everyone get the most out of the group experience. For example, most groups are most effective with ground rules like these:

- **Confidentiality:** What someone shares in the group stays in the group and is not repeated to outsiders for any reason.
- **Active Listening:** One of the best gifts you can give each other is your full attention. Listen closely to what others say in your group. Don't be focused on what you can say as soon as someone pauses. Think about what the other person is saying. Don't dominate the discussion.
- **No Distractions:** Silence and put away your phone.
- **Honesty:** Be honest about what you think.
- **Timeliness:** Arrive on time.
- **Commitment:** Try to commit to attending all six sessions of the group. If you can't attend, let the leader know.

As the leader, your primary job is to keep discussions on track with an eye on the clock to be sure you get through the whole session in ninety minutes. You may also need to keep the conversation shared fairly by drawing out quieter members and helping more talkative members to remember that others' insights are valued in your group.

It will be helpful if you preview the session's video teaching segment and then scan the discussion questions that pertain to it, highlighting various questions that you want to be sure to cover during your group's meeting. Ask God in advance of your time together to guide your group's discussion and then be sensitive to the direction He wishes to lead.

Ask group members to bring their study guide and pen to every meeting. Urge them to consider buying a copy of *The Rock, the Road, and the Rabbi* book by Kathie Lee Gifford to read along with this study.

BETHLEHEM

Where It All Began

So Joseph also went up from the town of Nazareth in Galilee to Judea, to Bethlehem the town of David, because he belonged to the house and line of David. He went there to register with Mary, who was pledged to be married to him and was expecting a child. While they were there, the time came for the baby to be born, and she gave birth to her firstborn, a son. She wrapped him in cloths and placed him in a manger, because there was no guest room available for them.

LUKE 2:4–7

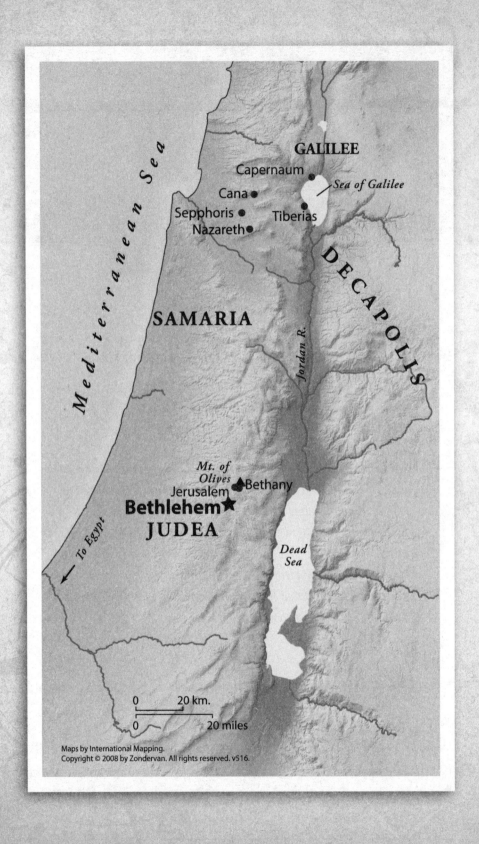

GALILEE

Capernaum

Sea of Galilee

Cana

Sepphoris

Tiberias

Nazareth

DECAPOLIS

Mediterranean Sea

SAMARIA

Jordan R.

Mt. of Olives

Jerusalem

Bethany

Bethlehem ★

JUDEA

To Egypt

Dead Sea

0   20 km.

0   20 miles

TODAY'S TOUR STOP

Ask someone in the group to read aloud this introduction to today's main setting: Bethlehem.

Jesus was born in Bethlehem, a small town about six miles south-southwest of Jerusalem. Today its population is about 25,000, mainly Palestinian Arabs, most of whom are Muslim, though there is a sizeable Palestinian Christian community. It is surrounded by major Jewish settlements of some 170,000 people. But in Jesus' day, Bethlehem was a Jewish town with a population of fewer than a thousand people, and maybe as few as one hundred.[1]

Bethlehem was important as the birthplace of King David, who lived a thousand years before Jesus. There was a prophecy that the Messiah, a descendant of David, would be born in Bethlehem. The Messiah was expected to be a godly military leader like David, who would drive out the foreign oppressors that controlled the Holy Land. At the time of Jesus' birth, His homeland was ruled by a nominal Jew, Herod the Great, who ignored God's law and collaborated with the hated Romans.

In this first session, we will travel to Bethlehem to see what happened there during the time of Herod the Great. We will explore the drama behind the Christmas carols about the little town of Bethlehem.

FIRST THOUGHTS

If you or any of your fellow group members do not know one another, take a few minutes to introduce yourselves. Then have each person in the group share an answer to these questions:

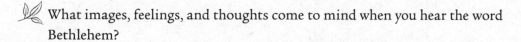 What images, feelings, and thoughts come to mind when you hear the word Bethlehem?

What do you hope to get out of this study of the Gospels and the Holy Land?

WATCH THE VIDEO

Watch the video segment for session one, which you can access by playing the DVD or through streaming. As you watch, use the outline below to record any thoughts or concepts that stand out to you.

Notes

We tend to picture Jesus as being born in a stable, but the evidence suggests He was born in a cave—the birthing place of lambs.

Jewish tradition tells us the animals born around the fields in Bethlehem were used as sacrifices in the temple for the worship of the Lord.

The caves were kept in a state of ritual purity, and the lambs were wrapped in swaddling cloth to keep them without spot or blemish.

Jesus was wrapped like one of these baby lambs to show that He is the Lamb of God who takes away the sins of the world.

Priestly garments too worn for use were made into the wicks of the menorah in the temple, which points to Jesus as the light of the world.

Every event in Jesus' life revolves around a Jewish holiday—He died as the Passover Lamb; His resurrection was on the Feast of Firstfruits; He poured out His spirit on Pentecost.

Bethlehem is about eighty miles from Nazareth. The town is mentioned in Scripture as the place where Jacob buried Rachel (see Genesis 35:19), where Ruth met Boaz (see Ruth 1:22–2:6), and where David was raised and anointed by the prophet Samuel (see 1 Samuel 16:1–13). It would have taken about four days for a person on foot or with a donkey to cover the distance from Bethlehem to Nazareth. Luke tells us that Mary and Joseph traveled to there to enroll in a census for tax purposes (see 2:1–5).[2]

When Joseph and Mary arrived, "the time came for the baby to be born" (verse 6). Mary "wrapped him in cloths and placed him in a manger, because there was no guest room available" (verse 7). A manger was a feeding trough for animals. Swaddling cloths were strips of fabric in which the baby was wrapped to immobilize his arms and legs to give him more restful sleep. The guest room (Greek *kataluma*) was likely a personal residence. The same term is used in Luke 22:11, where Jesus instructs His disciples, "Say to the owner of the house, 'The Teacher asks: Where is the *guest room*, where I may eat the Passover with my disciples?'"[3] Since there was no room like this available, Jesus was likely born in a cave.

After Jesus' birth, Luke reports that He was visited by "shepherds living out in the fields nearby" (2:8). Levitical shepherds were shepherds from the priestly tribe of Levi. They were responsible for making sure the newborn lambs to be used as sacrifices in the temple were without spot or blemish and did not contract any defects. Many scholars believe these shepherds swaddled newborn lambs to prevent them from such injury.

DEBRIEFING THE TOUR

Take a few minutes with your group members to discuss what you just watched and explore these concepts in Scripture.

1. What caught your attention most as you viewed the video?

2. Ask for a volunteer to read aloud Luke 2:1–18. (Because it is long, you could change readers every few paragraphs.) Jesus was born in the humblest of places: a cave for animals. In what ways did His humility reveal His greatness?

3. What explanations did Rabbi Sobel give in the video for why Jesus was:

    • Placed in a manger in a cave?

- Wrapped in swaddling cloths?

4. Why is it significant that Jesus may have been born in the same place as the lambs used for sacrifice in the temple?

5. What is the significance of the infant Jesus being wrapped in cloth that came from used priestly garments?

6. Take a few moments to review the information about the Feast of Tabernacles on the following page. What do you think about the idea that Jesus may have been born in September on the Feast of Tabernacles, rather than on December 25?

TRYING IT OUT

This is a hands-on activity to help you fix in your mind something you've learned in this session. For this activity, you will need cardboard, felt tip pens, white ribbon, and tape.

A crèche is a scene of the nativity, the birth of Jesus. Many Christians set up crèches at Christmastime to help them imagine the wonderful event in Bethlehem. Crèches can be made of wood, pottery, or many other materials. As a way of making the events more real to the members of your group, you can make a simple crèche together.

On sheets of cardboard, draw pictures of Mary, Joseph, the baby Jesus, a manger, shepherds, sheep, and a lamb. Make the adult figures at least six inches tall and the other figures in proportion to them. Cut out the figures. You may color or laminate them if you like. Tape additional wedges of cardboard onto the backs of Mary, Joseph, the shepherds, and the sheep so the figures can stand up. Use white ribbon to swaddle the baby Jesus and the lambs. Arrange your figures the way you imagine them in the cave at Bethlehem.

Another idea to try: buy or borrow a crèche, a nativity scene, to display in your home at Christmastime. Be sure to get some sheep with your crèche. When you display it, wrap the baby Jesus in strips of old cloth (linen would have been used in His day, but cotton will serve just as well). Also, wrap one of the sheep in strips of cloth to represent the young lambs that would have been swaddled there. Let this be a visual reminder of what you've learned about Jesus' birth.

The Feast of Tabernacles (also known as the Feast of Booths and Sukkot) commemorates the wandering of the Israelites in the desert after God liberated them from slavery in Egypt. It is the seventh feast that God commanded His people to observe in Leviticus 23. It is also one of three feasts the Jewish people were to observe each year by traveling to "the place [God] will choose" (Deuteronomy 16:16), which became Jerusalem.

The Feast of Tabernacles takes place on the 15th of the Hebrew month Tishri. This is the seventh month on the Hebrew calendar and usually occurs in late September to mid-October. The Jewish people would build temporary structures made from the branches of trees (called *sukkot* in Hebrew), much like those the Israelites lived in during their wandering, and live in them during the holiday. The feast lasted for eight days, beginning and ending with a Sabbath day of rest.[4]

The Feast of Tabernacles commemorates how God provided manna from heaven to feed the Israelites, water from the stones to quench them, and a pillar of cloud by day and fire by night to guide them. Ultimately, it reflects God's presence, provision, and protection for His people. And for Christians, it reminds us of the time when "the Word became flesh and made his dwelling among us [literally, tabernacled among us]" (John 1:14).

THAT'S A WRAP

This week, you and your group members learned some insights about Jesus' birth from Jewish tradition. You learned what Luke may have meant when he wrote in his Gospel about Jesus being wrapped in swaddling cloths and laid in a manger. As you prepare for personal study time this week, reflect on the truth that even from His birth, Jesus was destined to be our Passover Lamb without blemish, born to die to free us from sin and death.

CLOSING PRAYER

Father of grace, we thank You for sending Your Son into the world to be our Passover Lamb. Thank You that through His coming in the flesh, He has dealt with sin and death for all who trust in Him. We offer ourselves completely to You and ask You to be active and real in our lives this week. Please fill us with courage to face whatever comes to us during the coming week as we keep our eyes fixed on the Lamb. In Jesus' name, Amen.

RECOMMENDED READING

Read chapters 5 and 6 of *The Rock, the Road, and the Rabbi.*

DIGGING DEEPER

In this session, you traveled to the town of Bethlehem and explored the events that led to Jesus, the Messiah, being born there during the time of Herod the Great. The prophet Micah (c. 750–686 BC) had foretold that the Messiah would come from this humble village: "But you, Bethlehem Ephrathah, though you are small among the clans of Judah, out of you will come for me one who will be ruler over Israel, whose origins are from of old, from ancient times" (5:2). This personal study section will offer you some additional Bible passages to dig into on your own to enrich your study of this session's themes. Explore them all or select those that appeal to you.

DAY ONE

 Read Matthew 2:1–18. Why would Herod have been disturbed by the birth of someone whom the Magi called king of the Jews?

 How did Herod try to deal with the problem?

 How did God outwit Herod?

The "Magi" mentioned in Matthew 2:1 were likely followers of a Persian religion called Zoroastrianism. They were astronomers/astrologers who saw signs in the heavens about many things. We don't know how many of them went to worship the king of the Jews. Western tradition sets their number at three because of the three gifts they brought. Their importance is that they were non-Jews who recognized that the king of the Jews was going to be a significant figure for non-Jews as well.[5]

🌿 How does the slaughter of the innocent children in Bethlehem affect your view of the Christmas story?

🌿 Consider that the non-Jewish magi went to worship the king of the Jews. Why might this be important to you?

🌿 King Herod was a rich and powerful man during his lifetime. How does our culture urge us to admire and envy people like him?

🌿 List some concrete steps we can take to resist this influence.

The most central element of the Seder [Passover meal] in the first century was the Passover lamb. The command to eat the Passover lamb is first found in Exodus 12:8, which states: "They are to eat the meat that night, roasted over a fire. With *matzot* and bitter herbs they are to eat it" (TLV). The offering of the Passover lamb was meant to be a reminder of blood placed on the doorposts of the Israelites' homes in Egypt.

But not just any lamb would be acceptable to be eaten in fulfillment of the commandment of Passover. The Passover lamb had to be slaughtered as a sacrifice to the Lord (*korban*, in Hebrew), in the designated location that had been chosen for offerings. Deuteronomy 16:5–6 states: "You may not sacrifice the Passover offering within any of your gates that ADONAI your God is giving you. Rather, at the place ADONAI your God chooses to make His Name dwell, there you will sacrifice the Passover offering in the evening at sunset—the time of your coming out from Egypt" (TLV).

Since the destruction of the second Jerusalem temple by the Romans in AD 70, there has been no Passover sacrifice offered in the fulfillment of this prophecy. For this reason, Jews of European descent don't eat lamb today and will not do so until the temple in Jerusalem is restored.

Jesus taught that He was the true Passover lamb and the promised Messiah who came to bring about a greater Exodus. Moses came to redeem Israel from slavery in Egypt, but Messiah Jesus came to bring deliverance from sin and death. From the perspective of the New Testament, true freedom is found in God's Son, Jesus, of whom it is written, "If the Son sets you free, you will be free indeed!" (John 8:36 TLV).

God the Father sent His Son, Jesus, so that everyone who receives and believes in Him might find freedom and everlasting life in the world to come! Just like Israel had to apply the blood of the Passover lamb to the doorposts of their homes so that death would pass over their firstborn sons, so everyone of us must apply the blood of Jesus, the greater Passover Lamb of God, so that death and judgment will pass over us![6]

— From *The Rock, the Road, and the Rabbi*

DAY TWO

 To deepen your understanding of Jesus as the Passover lamb, read Exodus 12:1–13. This passage takes place while Moses is attempting to free the descendants of Jacob/Israel from slavery in Egypt. The passage contains the Old Testament law's instructions for the Passover lamb. What do you learn from this passage that sheds light on what Jesus accomplished for us as our Passover lamb?

 Why do you think it was so important that the sacrificed lamb was unblemished? How does this correlate to Jesus?

 What do you think was the point of putting blood on the doorframe of the family's house? How does this correlate to Jesus?

 What additional insights into Jesus as our Passover lamb do you glean from Rabbi Sobel's teaching from the book excerpt on the opposing page?

 What are some differences these insights will make in the way you live?

How have you experienced the freedom that Rabbi Sobel speaks of?

 Who can you tell about Jesus, your Passover lamb?

The Gospel writers intentionally used terms that were in current use in the Roman Empire when they were writing. For example, Augustus Caesar—the emperor at the time of Jesus' birth—was proclaimed on coins and monuments to be "the son of God" because his adoptive father, Julius Caesar, had been declared to be divine. The "gospel" was the good news that Augustus had brought peace on earth through his reign (by the power of the Roman army enforcing the peace). Augustus was called "Savior" and "Lord." There was a cult of Augustus by which people offered a pinch of incense in homage to him. They were encouraged to have "faith" in his promise to bring security and prosperity. The Gospel writers applied these words to Jesus to show that He was the true Lord who should be worshiped and that no Christian should place allegiance in a worldly empire.[7]

DAY THREE

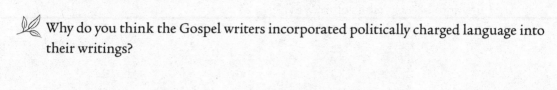 Why do you think the Gospel writers incorporated politically charged language into their writings?

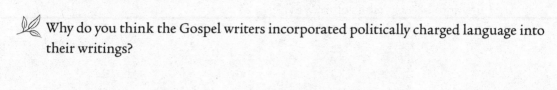 What does this tell you about their view of the Roman Empire and its claim that its emperors were divine?

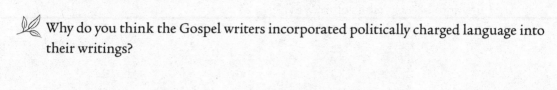 How do you think we are meant to relate to our own government's leaders in light of what the Bible claims about Jesus?

Do you tend to appreciate the role of the government (national, state, and local) in your life or to be suspicious of it? Why?

Offer to Jesus your praise as the one and only rightful ruler of heaven and earth.

REFLECT

Reflect on these points as you close out this week's personal study.

- Jesus was born in a stable or a cave where animals were kept. He was wrapped in strips of cloth and placed in a feeding trough for animals. It was not a glorious entrance into this world! Reflect on the significance of Jesus' birth and the circumstances surrounding His arrival as it relates to your understanding of who Jesus is.

- Consider the explanation of the Passover, the Passover lamb, and the Jewish tradition of Passover. Reflect on what these mean in your life today.

- Reflect on the kingdom God established and the role you play in it. Think about how your role in the God's kingdom intersects with your role in earthly "kingdoms."

NAZARETH

The Early Years

*So [Joseph] got up, took the child and his mother and went to
the land of Israel. But when he heard that Archelaus was
reigning in Judea in place of his father Herod, he was afraid to
go there. Having been warned in a dream, he withdrew to the
district of Galilee, and he went and lived in a town called
Nazareth. So was fulfilled what was said through the prophets,
that he would be called a Nazarene.*

MATTHEW 2:21—23

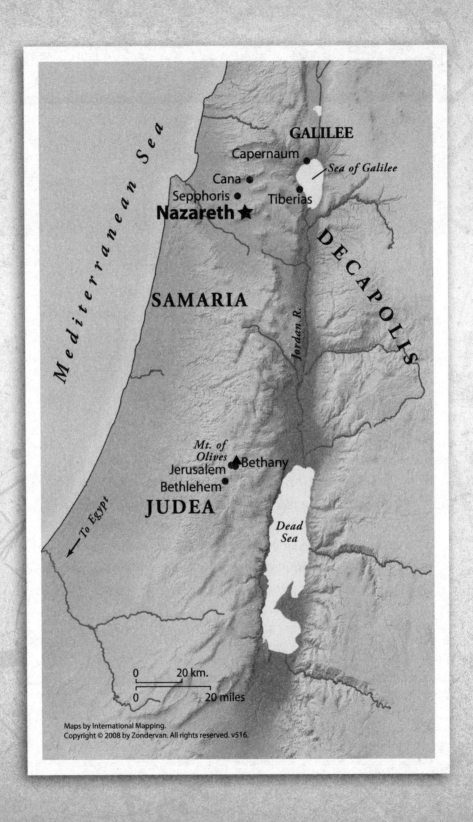

GALILEE

Capernaum

Sea of Galilee

Cana

Sepphoris

Tiberias

Nazareth

Mediterranean Sea

DECAPOLIS

SAMARIA

Jordan R.

*Mt. of
Olives*

Bethany

Jerusalem

Bethlehem

JUDEA

*Dead
Sea*

To Egypt

0   20 km.

0   20 miles

TODAY'S TOUR STOP

Ask someone in the group to read aloud this introduction to today's main setting: Nazareth.

After Jesus was born in Bethlehem, an angel appeared to Joseph and said, "Get up . . . take the child and his mother and escape to Egpyt. Stay there until I tell you, for Herod is going to search for the child to kill him" (Matthew 2:13). So Joseph and Mary took Jesus to Egypt for several years and stayed there until it was safe for them to return to their homeland. When they returned, they settled in Nazareth, located eighty miles north of Bethlehem, and Jesus lived there until He began His ministry at the age of thirty.

Nazareth was a village of probably fewer than five hundred people.[8] However, about a mile away was the cosmopolitan city of Sepphoris, with its Roman theater and mixed Jewish and non-Jewish population. Some part of Sepphoris was burned during Jesus' youth, and some scholars think Jesus—who was in the building trade in His teens and twenties—may have worked on the reconstruction of Sepphoris. There was certainly money in Sepphoris, money controlled by the friends of Herod Antipas, the son of Herod the Great.[9]

In this session, we will explore what Jesus' life was like when He was around thirty years old and just transitioning from His time as a builder to His time as a teacher. We will think about His situation in Nazareth, His pilgrimage to the Judean desert just before the start of His ministry, and His first miracle at the village of Cana.

FIRST THOUGHTS

Have each person in the group share an answer to these questions:

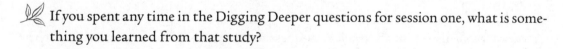 If you spent any time in the Digging Deeper questions for session one, what is something you learned from that study?

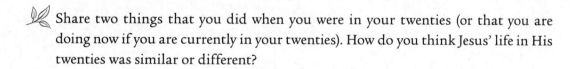 Share two things that you did when you were in your twenties (or that you are doing now if you are currently in your twenties). How do you think Jesus' life in His twenties was similar or different?

WATCH THE VIDEO

Play the video segment for session two. As you watch, use the outline below to record any thoughts or concepts that stand out to you.

Notes

The word for what Joseph and Jesus did as an occupation is *tektōn*, which means builder, craftsman, or architect.

The word *tektōn* points to Jesus as the *architect* of creation—"through the firstborn, God created the world."

The word *tektōn* also points to Jesus as the messianic craftsman, for in Jewish thought, the Messiah was going to be a craftsman (see Zechariah 1).

Messiah son of Joseph represents Jesus as the one rejected by his brothers, crucified on the cross, but ultimately exalted into a position of power.

Messiah son of David represents Jesus as the warrior king who is going to return to this earth to rule and reign.

Jesus' first miracle of turning the water into wine resembles the miracle performed through Moses of turning the Nile into blood—but whereas Moses brought judgment, Jesus came to bring abundant life.

[Bible scholar] Ray Vander Laan noted, "The word translated 'carpenter' in Matthew 13:55 and Mark 6:3 for how Joseph and Jesus made a living is the Greek word *tektōn*. It means 'builder.' You see, when the writers of the King James Version were translating the Greek into the English, they assumed, 'Oh, these guys were carpenters. Just like us.'

"The problem with that is that there were no trees that could be used for building in Israel at that time. . . . You see, there were only rocks in Israel. . . . Jesus was not a carpenter. Jesus was a stone mason." . . .

The Greek word *tektōn* can be translated as either "stone mason" or "architect." All these concepts are significant in reference to Jesus, since they connect back to Him as the architect of creation. . . .

Jesus is the *Tektōn*, the Architect of all creation. This reading aligns perfectly with the apostle John's understanding of creation. In John 1:3, he states, "Through him all things were made; without him nothing was made that has been made."[10]

—From *The Rock, the Road, and the Rabbi*

Debriefing the Tour

Take a few minutes with your group members to discuss what you just watched and explore these concepts in Scripture.

1. What caught your attention most as you viewed the video?

2. Ask for a volunteer to read Mark 6:1–3. This story took place when Jesus was thirty and had begun His ministry, traveling from village to village in the Galilee region, teaching and performing miracles. Finally, He went to His hometown and tried to teach there too. What do you learn from this passage about Jesus' life in Nazareth?

3. The word "carpenter" in Mark 6:3 in the Greek is *tektōn*, which means builder. As Kathie's tour guide (Ray Vander Laan) noted, in Israel, building was done with stone because there were few trees. So, Jesus was likely a stone mason, not a woodworker. Regardless of the specifics of His occupation, what does it tell you about Him?

4. What difference does it make to you that Jesus was the Architect of all creation? How does this affect your view of Him?

5. Have someone read aloud John 2:1–11, and then have someone read aloud the text about weddings on the next page. What connection did Rabbi Sobel draw between Jesus turning water into wine and Moses turning the Nile water into blood?

A wedding was a huge event for a Jewish village. The whole village would attend, and the celebration could go on for days. Running out of wine was a social calamity. But Jesus took advantage of the situation to teach His disciples an important lesson: The feast of the Messiah's coming had arrived. It was transforming the mere water of Jewish ceremonial washing into the excellent wine of God's kingdom. The Messiah had come! He had authority to upend Jewish rituals like washing and give them new meaning. The time for celebration was now.

6. What does the story in John 2:1–11 tell us about Jesus?

TRYING IT OUT

This is a hands-on activity to help you fix in your mind what you've learned in this session about Jesus' life in Nazareth. For this activity, you will need paper and pens. Alternatively, you could do your brainstorming on a whiteboard or flip chart.

Together, try to imagine what Jesus' life was like when He was a stone mason before He began His public ministry. Think about how He may have interacted with various people in His life: His family, His employers, His fellow workers, and even the Roman soldiers who were a constant presence in the towns where He would have worked. Brainstorm the

The Bible states that after Jesus was baptized in the Jordan River, initiating the start of His public ministry, He was led by the Holy Spirit into the wilderness, "where for forty days he was tempted by the devil" (Luke 4:1–2). Jesus returned to the region of the Galilee after this time to preach and teach the people who were living there. Luke notes, "He was teaching in their synagogues, and everyone praised him" (verse 15).

But this affirmation of Jesus' ministry changed when He returned to His hometown of Nazareth and, "as was his custom" (verse 16), went into the synagogue on the Sabbath and read from the scroll of Isaiah. Jesus applied the words of the prophet to Himself, saying, "Today this scripture is fulfilled in your hearing" (Luke 4:21). He then told the people—knowing they were looking for Him to perform miracles to support His claim—that "no prophet is accepted in his hometown" (verse 24).

The people became angry when Jesus then went on to describe how God sent the prophets Elijah and Elisha to the *Gentiles*. The kingdom of God that Jesus was announcing would be made available to all. Jesus was, in effect, telling the people of His hometown that they were no more worthy of God's love than anyone else and that they needed to humble themselves if they did not want to miss out on what God was doing.

Nazareth was situated among the ridges of the southern slopes of the Galilean hills, and when the people heard this, they took Jesus there to throw Him off and end His ministry. But it was not yet Jesus' time to die, and by some unexplained means, He made His way out. Today, you can visit a location in Israel called Mount Precipice (also known as Mount of the Leap of the Lord and Mount Kedumim), just outside the southern edge of Nazareth, where church tradition states this event took place.[11]

outline of a play in which Jesus interacts with one person or with a series of people. Have one group member write down your ideas until you have a vision for your play. For example, maybe Jesus interacts with a Roman soldier along the lines of Matthew 5:38–48. The soldier orders Jesus to carry his heavy pack for a mile. If you have enough time, assign roles to various group members and act out your play.

That's a Wrap

This week, you and your group members looked at two aspects of Jesus' early ministry: His life as a builder and His first miracle at the wedding in Cana. You were also invited to think about what it means that Jesus is the Architect of all creation. As you prepare for personal study time this week, try to wrap your mind around the two natures of Jesus the Messiah: His full humanness as He entered into our world, and His eternal divinity as the Son of God and Architect from before the foundation of our world.

Closing Prayer

Lord Jesus, we honor You as the Architect of the entire universe. We thank You that You changed the water of Jewish purification into the wine of Your kingdom. And we are humbled by Your willingness to live as an ordinary man, a stone mason, in a very specific time and place in history. Like Your first disciples, we have beheld Your glory and we want to follow where You lead. As we go through the coming week, enable us to notice and praise You for the work You have done designing the creation around us. We pray in Your great name, Amen.

Recommended Reading

Read chapters 7–8 and 10 of *The Rock, the Road, and the Rabbi.*

DIGGING DEEPER

In this session, you traveled to the village of Nazareth, located roughly fifty-fives north of Jerusalem, where Jesus lived until He began His ministry at around the age of thirty. Nazareth was an out-of-the-way place and not held in high esteem by the Jewish elite. Nathanael, one of Jesus' disciples, actually said, "Nazareth! Can anything good come from there?" (John 1:46) when told by Philip that Jesus was the Messiah. This personal study section will offer you additional Bible passages to dig into on your own to enrich your study of this session's themes. Explore them all or select those that appeal to you.

DAY ONE

Prior to Jesus beginning His ministry in Israel, the Holy Spirit led Him into the wilderness to be tempted by the devil. Jesus overcame the temptations by quoting Old Testament Scripture in reply to the enemy (Luke 4:1–13):

> "It is written: 'Man shall not live on bread alone.'"
> "It is written: 'Worship the Lord your God and serve him only.'"
> "It is said: 'Do not put the Lord your God to the test.'"

How might you use one of these verses to reject temptation? Or how might you use some other truth from Scripture, such as:

> "Get behind me, Satan!" (Matthew 16:23).
> "I am more than a conqueror because of Jesus Christ who loves me" (paraphrase of Romans 8:37).
> "I am a child of God, I am the offspring of the King, and therefore I am an heir to His kingdom! And just like Jesus, I still have work to do."

 Write down the verse or truth from Scripture that you want to take to heart, as well as the temptation you are rejecting.

 Has God ever led you into a desert experience to be tested? If so, what was your experience? What helped you to get through it?

In His teaching, Jesus twice referred to building with stone:

"On this rock I will build my church" (Matthew 16:18).
"The stone the builders rejected has become the cornerstone" (Psalm 118:22; Matthew 21:42).

 Look up these verses in context and identify in the space below what Jesus was intending to teach each time.

• Rock

• Stone

 How do these verses matter to you personally in your daily life?

The word *tektōn* can also be translated as "craftsman." The fact that the New Testament calls Jesus a *tektōn* is amazing, since Israel's Messiah is seen as a "craftsman," based upon the rabbinic understanding of Zechariah 2:1–4,[12] which says:

> Then I lifted up my eyes and behold, I saw four horns! I said to the angel speaking with me, "What are these?"
>
> He said to me, "These are the horns that have scattered Judah, Israel and Jerusalem."
>
> Then ADONAI showed me four craftsmen. I asked, "What are these coming to do?"
>
> He answered, "These are the horns that scattered Judah, so that no one could raise his head, but the craftsmen have come to frighten them, to cast down the horns of the nations that have lifted up their horn against the land of Judah to scatter it" (TLV).

Commenting upon the four craftsmen mentioned in Zechariah 2, the rabbis in Jewish tradition state: "Who are the four craftsmen? Messiah son of David, Messiah son of Joseph, Elijah, and the righteous [High] Priest, [who will serve in the messianic era]."[13]

Jesus is the messianic craftsman whom Zechariah spoke about. The mention of two Messiahs in this passage might seem confusing. But in Jewish thought, "Messiah son of Joseph" is the one who will suffer to redeem God's people, and "Messiah son of David" is the one who will defeat God's enemies to establish the messianic kingdom. So, while many Jews see these two roles being fulfilled by two separate individuals, the New Testament teaches that Jesus at His first coming came as Messiah son of Joseph, who suffered as the "Lamb of God, who takes away the sin of the world" (John 1:29), and at the Second Coming will reveal Himself as Messiah son of David, who will establish God's kingdom as the Lion of Judah.[14]

—From *The Rock, the Road, and the Rabbi*

Day Two

 Read the excerpt on the opposite page. Horns were a symbol of power in ancient Israel. What do the four craftsmen in Zechariah 1:20–21 represent?

 Twelve times in the New Testament, Jesus is referred to as the Son of David. The speakers are all clearly intending to identify Him as the Messiah. Five times He is called the son of Joseph—three of these are in a genealogy, and one of the others is an attempt to dismiss Him as a well-known man in Nazareth. What do these references suggest about the kind of messiah that His contemporaries were hoping He would be?

Jesus is the promised master craftsman and architect of creation who brings order out of chaos and *shalom* to our lives in this world and in the world to come! You don't have to wait to begin to experience His peace until His kingdom comes—you can have it right now as He promised: "*Shalom* I leave you, My *shalom* I give to you; but not as the world gives! Do not let your heart be troubled or afraid" (John 14:27 TLV).[15]

 Shalom is peace, wholeness, prosperity of the whole person. What does it mean to say that God offers you *shalom* here and now?

 How has Jesus brought order out of chaos?

 How can we participate in Jesus' mission of bringing order out of chaos?

DAY THREE

 Let's dig deeper into Jesus' first miracle of turning water into wine at Cana found in John 2:1–12. What is the emptiness in your life that God wants to transform into fullness? (Ask Him to do that.)

 How has He already brought fullness into your life? (Thank Him for that.)

Jesus' first miracle is symbolic of what the Lord wants to do in you. Like the water into wine, God wants to transform you from ordinary to extraordinary. In Messiah you are a new creation: "the old has gone, the new is here!" (2 Corinthians 5:17). Ask God today to transform any emptiness in your life into fullness.

Jesus performed His miracle at a wedding in Cana of Galilee. But of all the miracles Jesus could have performed, why was His first recorded miracle turning water into wine? To answer this question, we must understand John's purpose for writing his Gospel, which was to demonstrate that "Jesus is the Messiah, the Son of God" (John 20:31). The Messiah, according to the Torah and Jewish tradition, was going to be greater than Moses, as the Lord states in Deuteronomy 18:18: "I will raise up for them a prophet like you [Moses] from among their fellow Israelites, and I will put my words in his mouth. He will tell them everything I command him."

What was the first miracle Moses performed to demonstrate to Israel and Pharaoh that he was the redeemer sent by God to deliver them? He turned water into blood. But Jesus, the greater Moses, turned water into wine because He did not come to bring death, but so that we might have life and have it more abundantly (John 10:10).

Wine is the one of the primary signs of the abundant blessings of the coming messianic kingdom. The messianic prophecy in Amos 9:13 states, "The mountains will drip sweet wine and all the hills will melt over" (TLV); the one in Isaiah 25:6 says, "On this mountain, ADONAI-Tzva'ot will prepare a lavish banquet for all peoples—a banquet of aged wine—of rich food, of choice marrow, of aged wine well refined" (TLV). By turning the water into wine, Jesus demonstrated that He was the promised prophet, the greater Moses, who came that we might begin to experience the abundant life of the messianic kingdom here and now through faith in Messiah Jesus.[16]

—From *The Rock, the Road, and the Rabbi*

🌿 God's first miracle through Moses in Egypt was turning the water of the Nile into blood. This was a warning to Pharaoh and the Egyptians that Israel's God had the power of death. Why, then, was turning water into wine an appropriate first sign from Jesus? What did it point toward?

🌿 What does it look like to experience the abundant life of the kingdom here and now?

🌿 How do you deal with the already-but-not-yet quality of the kingdom abundance? What helps you?

REFLECT

Reflect on these points as you close out this week's personal study.

- Do you tend to lean more toward thinking of Jesus as a man, or more toward thinking of Him as God, or do you think you keep both aspects of Him in a good balance? Why did you answer the way you did?

- Reflect on John 2:11. How does this verse reveal the glory of God through Jesus?

- Consider and pray about the abundance we are waiting to receive when Jesus' kingdom comes in its fullness.

CAPERNAUM

Ministry Headquarters

Then he went down to Capernaum, a town in Galilee, and on the Sabbath he taught the people. They were amazed at his teaching, because his words had authority. . . . Jesus left the synagogue and went to the home of Simon. Now Simon's mother-in-law was suffering from a high fever, and they asked Jesus to help her. So he bent over her and rebuked the fever, and it left her. She got up at once and began to wait on them.

LUKE 4:31–32, 38–39

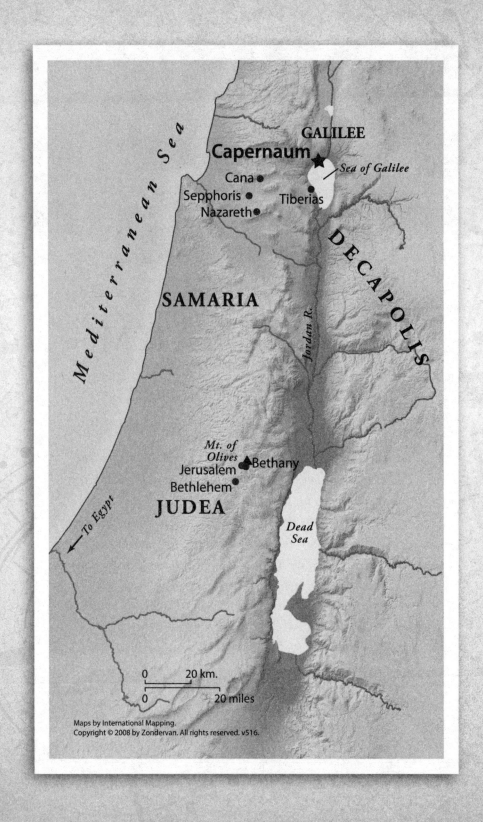

GALILEE

Capernaum

Sea of Galilee

Cana

Sepphoris

Nazareth

Tiberias

Mediterranean Sea

DECAPOLIS

SAMARIA

Jordan R.

Mt. of Olives

Jerusalem   Bethany

Bethlehem

JUDEA

To Egypt

Dead Sea

0   20 km.

0   20 miles

TODAY'S TOUR STOP

Ask someone in the group to read aloud this introduction to today's setting: Capernaum.

The village of Capernaum became Jesus' headquarters when He became a rabbi (teacher) at the age of thirty. Capernaum sits on the northwest coast of the Sea of Galilee. In Jesus' day, it probably covered less than twenty-five acres and housed 600 to 1,500 people.[17] Like most villages in the area, its homes were built of basalt, a black stone, and probably roofed with mud and reeds. Fishing was the main local enterprise.

Because it sits on a major trade route, Capernaum made sense as a headquarters for a ministry that involved traveling around the Galilee region, visiting synagogues on the Sabbath, and teaching in the open air on other days of the week. Jesus' followers were literally the people who followed Him from village to village to hear His teaching that carried a ring of authority and to see Him perform wonders of healing and casting out demons.

In this session, we will visit Capernaum to see some of what Jesus said and did there as He began His ministry as a rabbi. We will learn what rabbis did and also consider what Jesus did that set Him apart from typical rabbis.

FIRST THOUGHTS

Have each person in the group share an answer to these questions:

 If you spent any time in the Digging Deeper questions for session two, what is something you learned from that study?

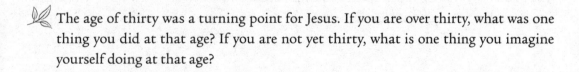 The age of thirty was a turning point for Jesus. If you are over thirty, what was one thing you did at that age? If you are not yet thirty, what is one thing you imagine yourself doing at that age?

WATCH THE VIDEO

Play the video segment for session three. As you watch, use the outline below to record any thoughts or concepts that stand out to you.

Notes

The rabbis would travel the countryside gathering disciples, preaching and teaching the people as they went along, and then teach on the *shabbat* (day of rest).

By using the number *490* when instructing Peter how many times to forgive, Jesus was saying that his faith could not be complete if he was not willing to wholeheartedly forgive.

The number *490* is also the numeric value for Bethlehem, which is significant because Jesus was born that we might find forgiveness.

Just as a person cannot live physically without "bread," we cannot live spiritually and emotionally without forgiveness.

Forgiveness is the key that sets us free, and it is what sets other people free as well.

When we build our lives on the Lord, the Word, and faith, we create a legacy that stands for generations to come.

The role of the rabbi in the Jewish faith is central to understanding the Jewish people. Rabbis were trained to be "good shepherds" to the common people who, like sheep, were simple-minded and in desperate need of leadership. The word *rabbi* means "teacher," and because most people in first-century Israel were uneducated in a formal sense, it was left to the rabbis to explain the fundamentals of the faith to the needy, seeking, often confused individuals who followed them on their travels.

The rabbi would often begin by simply commanding, "Come!" and the people would follow and begin their journey with him. It was understood that the people were never to ask, "Where are we going?" or "What are you going to teach us when we get there?" . . . Furthermore, rabbis in the first century were aware that the people who listened to them were uneducated, peasant folk for the most part. So the rabbi typically spoke of things the average person could understand through their senses.

Teaching in parables was an art form of communication at the most primal level, and nobody did it better than Jesus. Out in a field, you can picture Jesus pointing and saying, "Consider the lilies of the field, how they grow" (Matthew 6:28 NKJV). There are flowers everywhere in Israel. But instead of lilies as we envision them, they are more like huge red poppies dominating the landscape. They are just gorgeous! . . .

Jesus knew the longing in the people's hearts to understand the truths He was teaching them. And He loved the purity of their desire to know their Father more intimately. They needed hope, and Jesus delivered hope to them on a daily basis for the next three years.[18]

—From *The Rock, the Road, and the Rabbi*

DEBRIEFING THE TOUR

Take a few minutes with your group members to discuss what you just watched and explore these concepts in Scripture.

1. What caught your attention most as you viewed the video?

2. Ask for a volunteer to read aloud Mark 1:14–39. (Because it is longer passage, you might want to change readers every few paragraphs.) In this passage, how was Jesus like other rabbis of His day?

3. How was Jesus different from other rabbis?

4. What do you think Jesus meant when He said, "The kingdom of God has come near" (verse 15)?

5. What do you think Jesus' habit of driving out demons told the people of Capernaum about the kingdom of God?

6. In this passage from Mark, Jesus teaches more by action than by word. What effect do you think this would have had on people?

TRYING IT OUT

This is a hands-on activity to help you fix in your mind how effective and vivid Jesus' rabbinic teaching was. For this activity, you will need paper and felt tip pens or pencils.

Matthew 13 contains seven of Jesus' parables, the stories He told as He taught the crowds. To get a feel for how visual and concrete (rather than abstract and intellectual) they are, try drawing them. Choose a parable from the following list:

- Matthew 13:1–9 (the farmer sowing seed)
- Matthew 13:24–30 (the weeds)
- Matthew 13:31–32 (the mustard seed)

- Matthew 13:33 (the yeast)
- Matthew 13:44 (hidden treasure)
- Matthew 13:45–46 (the pearl)
- Matthew 13:47–50 (the net)

It's fine for two group members to draw the same parable. It's also fine to draw just a portion of the parable or one important item from the parable. Think about how your parable launches from the everyday life that would have been familiar to Jesus' first hearers. Take about ten minutes to draw, and then share your drawing with the group.

THAT'S A WRAP

This week, you and your group members looked at the first chapter of Mark's Gospel to see what kind of teacher Jesus was. You also had the chance to draw something from one of Jesus' parables to get a feel for how visual and concrete they are. As you prepare for personal study time this week, think about Jesus as your teacher, a teacher with authority in your life. Look for the ways He teaches you not just in your study time but also as you go through your day. Be alert for His concrete lessons through your experiences.

CLOSING PRAYER

Jesus, You are our Rabbi. You are our Teacher. We acknowledge Your authority and we want to follow where You lead. Go before each one of us this week and open our ears to those moments when You say, "Come!" Help us to become aware of Your kingdom, the realm where what You want done is done gladly and without resistance. We want to be part of that. In Your name of authority we pray, Amen.

RECOMMENDED READING

Read chapter 11 of *The Rock, the Road, and the Rabbi.*

DIGGING DEEPER

In this session, you traveled to the village of Capernaum, located on the northwestern shore of the Sea of Galilee. The Bible states that five of Jesus' disciples hailed from this small town. Peter (known as Simon at the time) and Andrew were brothers, as were James and John. All four were fishermen on the Sea of Galilee before following Jesus' call. Matthew, the other disciple from Capernaum, was a tax collector. This personal study section will offer you additional Bible passages to dig into on your own to enrich your study of this session's themes. Explore them all or select those that appeal to you.

DAY ONE

 Rabbi Sobel noted that at Capernaum, Jesus told Peter to forgive up to 490 times. He then went on to list Hebrew words and phrases whose numerical equivalent was 490. What do the following words add to your understanding about why forgiving others is so important for Christians?

- Hebrew *tamim* = English "complete," "perfect," or "finished." "A person who can't forgive will always live an imperfect and incomplete life that lacks a true understanding of the 'finished,' gracious work of the cross."

- Hebrew *moladati* = English "my nativity"

- Hebrew *Beit Lechem* = English "Bethlehem," "House of Bread." "Jesus was born so that we might be forgiven. And forgiveness is associated with bread in the Lord's Prayer, which says: 'Give us this day our daily bread. And forgive us our debts as we also have forgiven our debtors' (Matthew 6:11–12 TLV). Just like a person can't live without their daily bread, an individual can't survive without forgiveness."

 Have you experienced forgiveness? If so, write down a few of the things for which you have been forgiven.

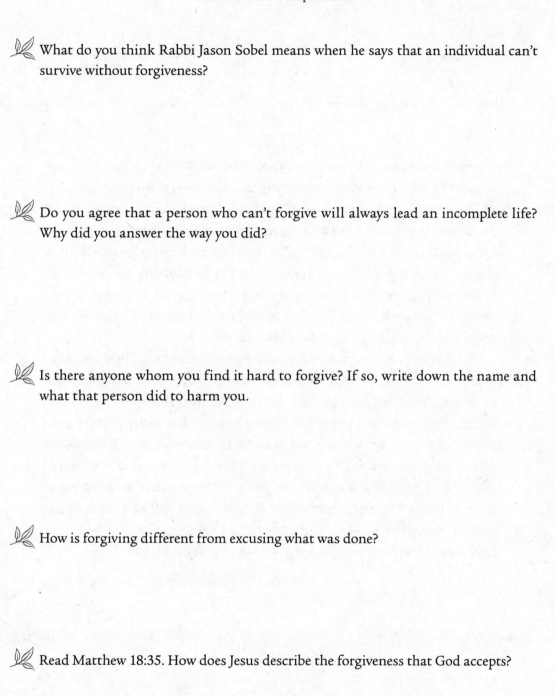

What do you think Rabbi Jason Sobel means when he says that an individual can't survive without forgiveness?

Do you agree that a person who can't forgive will always lead an incomplete life? Why did you answer the way you did?

Is there anyone whom you find it hard to forgive? If so, write down the name and what that person did to harm you.

How is forgiving different from excusing what was done?

Read Matthew 18:35. How does Jesus describe the forgiveness that God accepts?

The psalmist wrote, "If you, LORD, kept a record of sins, Lord, who could stand?" (Psalm 130:3). We need to learn to forgive and to be forgiven. How do we celebrate the forgiveness Messiah has brought us? By partaking of the broken bread of the Lord's Supper, concerning which Jesus said, "This is my body given for you; do this in remembrance of me" (Luke 22:19). Jesus, who is the Bread of Life, was born in Bethlehem, the House of Bread, so that we might both experience forgiveness and extend the bread of forgiveness to others. When we fail to forgive, it's like we are spiritually withholding food from a starving person!

Forgiveness is not an elective; it is a requirement for Christians. We must forgive because we have been forgiven by the Lord. Extending forgiveness should not even be dependent on receiving an apology, as Paul wrote: "Bear with each other and forgive one another if any of you has a grievance against someone. Forgive as the Lord forgave you" (Colossians 3:13). For this reason, forgiveness is one of the greatest acts of faith and a true sign of faithfulness to the Lord. We must forgive because we have been forgiven. The practical benefit of forgiveness is that it frees us as well as the other person. Unforgiveness keeps you imprisoned and chained to your past, but forgiving is a key that sets you free.[19]

—From *The Rock, the Road, and the Rabbi*

DAY TWO

 Read the excerpt on the opposite page. How do you respond to the idea that forgiveness is a requirement for Christians?

 As you read Paul's words in Colossians 3:13, how do you define what it means to "bear with each other?" What makes that difficult to do in your life?

 What does it mean to "forgive as the Lord forgave you"?

In what ways does unforgiveness keep you chained to your past?

 What are some pratical benefits of forgiving others?

Do you need to forgive someone in your life? If so, write a letter to that person that you will *not* send. This will be just for you. Write out what the offense was, without either minimizing it or overdramatizing it. Tell how it has affected you. Then write that you forgive the person and let go of all desire that he or she pay for what was done.

This is the crucial part of forgiveness: we let God be responsible for punishment and we let go of our desire to see to it that punishment happens.

Not yet ready to forgive? Write a letter to God explaining the offense and expressing your emotions over it. Be honest about your anger and other feelings. Then tell God what's keeping you from forgiving. Ask Him to help you to become willing to forgive.

Ask God to help you take a step closer to forgiving. Thank Him that He has forgiven all of your faults, including unforgiveness.

If you can't think of anyone in your life whom you haven't forgiven, then celebrate! Write a letter to God expressing gratitude for the the ways you've been forgiven and the ways that He has helped you to forgive.

Day Three

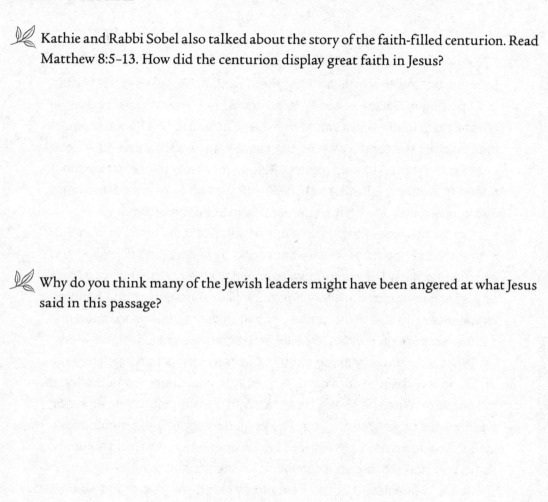 Kathie and Rabbi Sobel also talked about the story of the faith-filled centurion. Read Matthew 8:5–13. How did the centurion display great faith in Jesus?

Why do you think many of the Jewish leaders might have been angered at what Jesus said in this passage?

In what areas of life do you need to have faith like that of the centurion?

Scholars believe that in Jesus' day, there were no Roman legions posted in Capernaum. Galilee at the time belonged to Herod Antipas, a faithful client-king of Rome, and it would have been unsual for the Romans to post their soldiers in a territory where the client-king was loyal and no serious internal or external threats existed. Rather, it is likely the centurion mentioned in Matthew 8:5–13 and Luke 7:1–10 was an auxiliary posted there by Herod—a non-Jewish man perhaps from Lebanon or Syria.

Centurions were the principal professional officers in the ancient Roman army, serving as its military backbone by maintaining discipline and executing orders. The centurion was nominally the commander of a "century" (Latin *centuria*), a military unit originally consisting of one hundred legionaries. The size of the century changed over time, and from the first century BC through most of imperial era, it consisted of just eighty men.

What is noteworthy in the story of the centurion is that he clearly understood the chain of command. A centurion was under the authority of the emperor. When he spoke, he spoke with the authority of the emperor, and thus his order was obeyed. The centurion applied this same understanding to Jesus. He believed that Jesus was vested with God's authority, so he only needed to give a command for the servant to be healed.

Jesus was amazed at the centurion's response (see Matthew 8:10; Luke 7:9). Even though he was a Gentile, he had discerned the nature of Jesus' authority. This prompted Jesus to say of him, "I tell you, I have not found such great faith even in Israel" (Luke 7:9).[20]

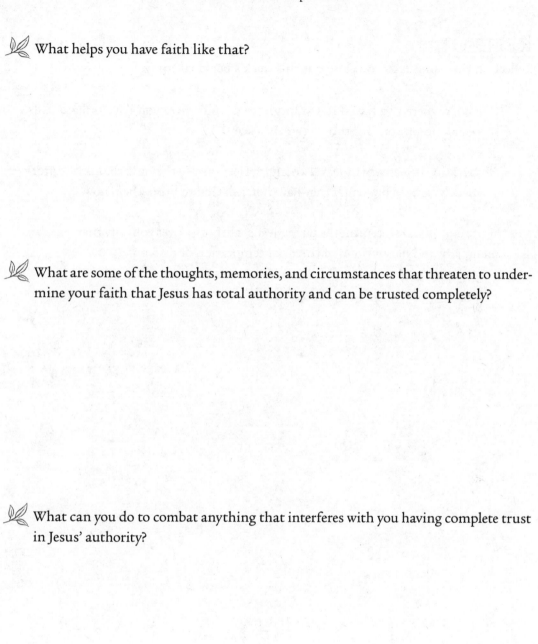 What helps you have faith like that?

What are some of the thoughts, memories, and circumstances that threaten to undermine your faith that Jesus has total authority and can be trusted completely?

What can you do to combat anything that interferes with you having complete trust in Jesus' authority?

REFLECT

Reflect on these points as you close out this week's personal study.

- Consider where you have known forgiveness and where you have offered it. Is there balance in your heart between the two?

- Go back to the activity in Day Two and reflect on whether any chains of unforgiveness have been broken. If they have not, ask God to break them now.

- Write a personal statement declaring Jesus' authority over your life that you can memorize and use in times of threat or temptation or discord.

GALILEE

Ministry Grounds

*Jesus went throughout Galilee, teaching in their synagogues,
proclaiming the good news of the kingdom, and healing every
disease and sickness among the people. News about him spread
all over Syria, and people brought to him all who were ill with
various diseases, those suffering severe pain, the demon-possessed,
those having seizures, and the paralyzed; and he healed them.
Large crowds from Galilee, the Decapolis, Jerusalem,
Judea and the region across the Jordan followed him.*

MATTHEW 4:23—25

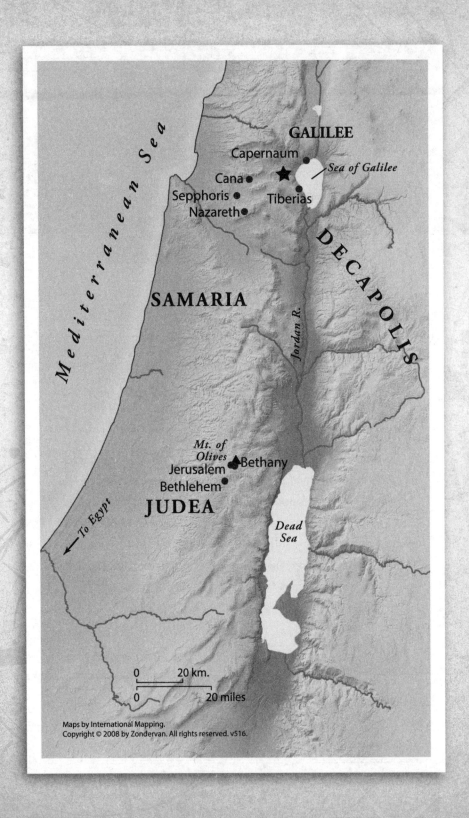

Mediterranean Sea

GALILEE

Capernaum

Cana

Sepphoris

Nazareth

Tiberias

Sea of Galilee

DECAPOLIS

SAMARIA

Jordan R.

Mt. of Olives

Bethany

Jerusalem

Bethlehem

JUDEA

To Egypt

Dead Sea

0   20 km.

0   20 miles

TODAY'S TOUR STOP

Ask someone in the group to read aloud this introduction to today's main setting: Galilee.

The Sea of Galilee is a freshwater lake, fourteen miles long and seven miles wide. To walk all the way around it is a thirty-three-mile trip. The Jews of Jesus' day lived on the west side of the lake, while the east side was largely populated by pagans whom the Jews regarded as unclean. There was a group of towns on the eastern side known as the Decapolis (Greek for "ten cities") that shared a similar language, culture, religion, and political status, with each functioning as an autonomous city-state dependent on the Roman Empire.

There was also a continuous band of settlement all along the west side of the lake where the Jews resided, mostly in the style of villages, although King Herod was building the city of Tiberias in the Roman style. While there were plenty of fishermen in boats along the shore, they avoided going out into the deep water at the center of the lake because of the danger of sudden storms that swept down from the mountains without notice and could easily capsize the small fishing boats the people used.

In this session, we will look at some stories in the Gospels that take place on or near the Sea of Galilee. We will see how Jesus' attitude toward everything from women to non-Jews to the lake itself was a shock to His followers.

FIRST THOUGHTS

Have each person in the group share an answer to these questions:

🌿 If you spent any time in the Digging Deeper questions from session three, what is something you learned from that study?

🌿 In Jesus' time, people were often cut off from society because of their afflictions, which is a common feeling for many teenagers today. Share a little bit about your own experience as a teen. Did you tend to feel shut out of the in-crowd, or did you fit in well with the people around you?

WATCH THE VIDEO

Play the video segment for session four. As you watch, use the outline below to record any thoughts or concepts that stand out to you.

Notes

Historically, the Jews were terrified of water—bad things happened on bodies of water—and even today they don't like to go out in it.

Jesus called His disciples to cross the Sea of Galilee (known by the Jews as "the abyss") and go to the pagan cities called the Decapolis.

The woman with the issue of blood was bold in touching Jesus' garment because it was immodest for a woman to touch a holy rabbi or any man outside of her own family.

The woman touched the tassels on the corners of Jesus' garment, which is symbolic of the power of God's Word to touch and heal our lives.

Women in the ancient world were treated like property, but Jesus allowed them to sit at His feet and learn, valuing them the same as the men who were around Him.

When Jesus told the disciples to cast their nets on the right side, He was telling them to "fish" from a place of kindness and love, not from a place of strict justice, legalism, or judgment.

It's difficult in our modern culture to imagine what life was like in Israel during the time of Jesus. The Jews experienced terrible suffering under Roman rule—physically, emotionally, and spiritually.

The Romans were brutal, violent oppressors who took every opportunity to whip their subjects into submission. They despised the Jewish faith and saw it as inferior to their polytheistic worldview. The Jews, in return, despised the Romans because of their oppressive taxes and their "unclean" culture and pagan religion. And more than anything, the Jews resented the Romans' absolute power over their daily life and worship.

Daily living for every Jew was an act of faith. They spent each waking moment trying to keep not only the Torah—the Mosaic law—but also the extra six-hundred-plus man-made laws imposed on them by the Pharisees and the Sadducees. We can't imagine the weight of such a legalistic burden on everyday life. No one could be pure enough, or holy enough, or without blemish before God under such self-righteous leaders. . . .

Jesus came to ease the burdens on the Jewish people. In Matthew 11:28, He said: "Come to me, all you who are weary and burdened, and I will give you rest." No wonder the people's hearts soared when they heard Him teach! No one in their world ever spoke such words of life or hope or compassion to them. Such love! Jesus' words still have the same effect today on those whose hearts are open to His tender message of grace.[21]

—From *The Rock, the Road, and the Rabbi*

DEBRIEFING THE TOUR

Take a few minutes with your group members to discuss what you just watched and explore these concepts in Scripture.

1. What caught your attention most as you viewed the video?

2. Ask for a volunteer to read aloud Luke 8:22–39. (Because it is long, you could take turns reading paragraphs.) What do we learn about Jesus from verses 22–25?

3. Why do you think Jesus' decision to go over to the non-Jewish side of the lake was shocking to His disciples?

4. What might life have been like for the formerly demonized man after he was healed?

5. Why do you think that Jesus did not allow the man go back to the Jewish side of the lake with Him?

6. Which of these two stories—the trip across the lake or the healing of the demonized man—is most relevant to your life? Why? What will you take away from this story?

TRYING IT OUT

This is a hands-on activity intended to take your closing prayer time to a higher level and help you connect with the way Jesus ministered to men and women.

Jesus traveled all the way across the Sea of Galilee just to heal one man. He cares about people whom no one else cares about. So today, think about how the group can pray for you. If you're not suffering from anything, how can the group pray for you to go deeper with God? Or how can the group give thanks for what's happening in your life?

People really experience being prayed for when you place your hands on them. It's easy to request prayer for other people and much deeper when you let the group pray for you in your own areas of need. With this in mind, gather around each person and pray for him or her. Place a hand on his or her shoulder. Ask God to heal this person, or to give him or her the courage to travel to the other side of the lake, or whatever else he or she needs.

THAT'S A WRAP

This week, you and your group members concentrated on one trip across the Sea of Galilee that revealed Jesus as having authority over the wind and waves as well as over demons. The goal has been to help you see Him as having authority in every area of your life and your world. It's one thing to know in your head that He has authority, but another thing to yield all attempts to control your world and put yourself totally at His disposal. As you prepare for your personal study time this week, think about the areas in your world that you have trouble completely yielding to Jesus.

Many scholars believe Jesus shared the parable of the prodigal son, recorded in Luke 15:11–32, while in Capernaum, just a few miles from the Decapolis, across the Sea of Galilee. In Jesus' day, the Decapolis was a Hellenistic (Greek-influenced) area, deeply entrenched in pagan worship and therefore forbidden to any Jew who wished to remain ritually clean, pure, or holy before God. In our vernacular, the setting of the parable would be as if a son left for Las Vegas—Sin City, baby! The prodigal succumbed to all the depravity that infamous mecca had to offer.

There is an ancient road that follows the coast of the Sea of Galilee from Capernaum to the Decapolis. In this parable, it is noteworthy that the father saw his son returning home from "a long way off" (Luke 15:20), picked up his robe, and ran for joy toward his precious "sin-soaked" son. In Jesus' day, the father's action would have shocked his audience. No decent Jewish man would be so immodest as to lift his robe, nor would he embarrass himself by running toward a son who had brought him so much shame. By all rights, the prodigal should have been dead to him. But the beauty of it is the exact opposite! His son was alive! He was coming home, and he was sorry! The father simply could not contain his glorious joy.

Of course, the father in this parable is a metaphor for God, our heavenly Father, and how He acts whenever one of us, His children, repents and returns. . . . The father in the story embraced his son with total abandon. . . . He treated him as royalty instead of what he actually was: an ingrate, a degenerate, and a profound disappointment to everyone.[22]

—From *The Rock, the Road, and the Rabbi*

CLOSING PRAYER

Lord Jesus, even the wind and the waves obey You. The demons obey You. So do the angels and every star and planet in the universe. You have graciously given us choices about whether and when we will obey You. It's hard for us to yield fully to You, even though we know You are the best King we could possibly have. Please help us to say yes to You throughout our lives. Please show us the areas we are holding back from You. In Your name of authority we pray, Amen.

RECOMMENDED READING

Read chapters 9, 12, and 14 of *The Rock, the Road, and the Rabbi.*

DIGGING DEEPER

In this session, you traveled to the region of Galilee, located on the western side of the Sea of Galilee, and looked at the story of Jesus healing a woman with an issue of blood after she touched the *tzitzit* of his garment. You also traveled to the eastern side of the lake, a place most Jewish people avoided called the Decapolis, where Jesus healed a demon-possessed man who had been living there among the tombs. This personal study section will offer you additional Bible passages to dig into on your own to enrich your study of this session's themes. Explore them all or select those that appeal to you.

The bleeding woman who approached Jesus in the crowd had every reason to be fearful. Among religious Jews, it was—and still is—considered immodest and inappropriate to touch a man, even one's husband, in public. But even worse, the woman was considered ceremonially unclean and could have spread her impurity to any person she touched.[23]

This is due to the laws in Leviticus 15 about bodily purity. These laws said a man's bodily discharge or a woman's discharge of blood made a person unclean for purposes of entering the Jewish temple and participating in the worship there. A person had to wait until the discharge ended and then go through a process of purification before he or she could enter the temple courts or touch anyone else who wanted to enter the temple.

The purpose of this law was to set the worship of the Lord apart from the customs of pagan worship. Blood and male seed were symbols of life, and pagan religions used them in their fertility rites. For example, all over the Roman world in Jesus' day, men had relations with prostitutes in temples in order to assure fertility of land, animals, and people.

God wanted to separate His people from all of that, so He gave them a series of purity laws to follow. Unfortunately, the teachers of the Jewish law had become so obsessed with these purity laws that they treated a bleeding woman as if she were morally unclean and disgusting.

DAY ONE

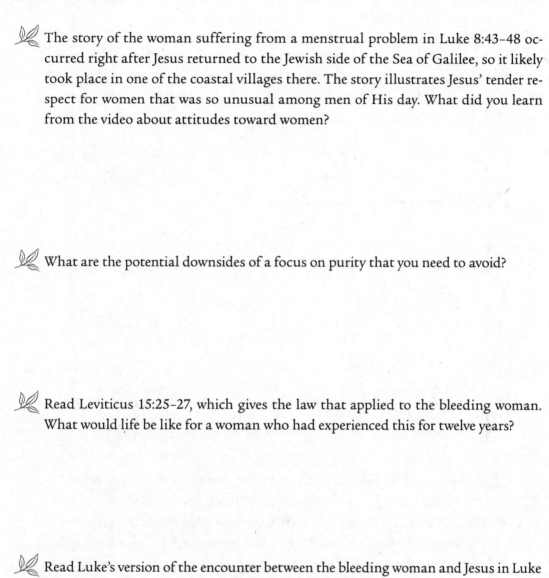

The story of the woman suffering from a menstrual problem in Luke 8:43–48 occurred right after Jesus returned to the Jewish side of the Sea of Galilee, so it likely took place in one of the coastal villages there. The story illustrates Jesus' tender respect for women that was so unusual among men of His day. What did you learn from the video about attitudes toward women?

What are the potential downsides of a focus on purity that you need to avoid?

Read Leviticus 15:25–27, which gives the law that applied to the bleeding woman. What would life be like for a woman who had experienced this for twelve years?

Read Luke's version of the encounter between the bleeding woman and Jesus in Luke 8:43–48. Why was the woman trembling with fear in verse 47?

How was Jesus' response to this woman in verse 48 different from what a typical rabbi would have done? What does this tell you about Him?

 What need drives you to lay hold of Jesus?

The LORD said to Moses, "Speak to the Israelites and say to them: 'Throughout the generations to come you are to make tassels on the corners of your garments, with a blue cord on each tassel. You will have these tassels to look at and so you will remember all the commands of the LORD, that you may obey them and not prostitute yourselves by chasing after the lusts of your own hearts and eyes. Then you will remember to obey all my commands and will be consecrated to your God. I am the LORD your God, who brought you out of Egypt to be your God. I am the LORD your God'" (Numbers 15:37–41).

DAY TWO

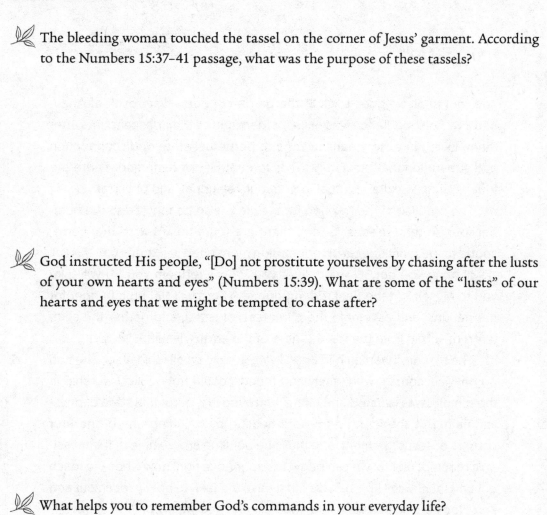 The bleeding woman touched the tassel on the corner of Jesus' garment. According to the Numbers 15:37–41 passage, what was the purpose of these tassels?

God instructed His people, "[Do] not prostitute yourselves by chasing after the lusts of your own hearts and eyes" (Numbers 15:39). What are some of the "lusts" of our hearts and eyes that we might be tempted to chase after?

What helps you to remember God's commands in your everyday life?

The root of all sin goes back to the garden of Eden. The result of Adam and Eve's disobedience was exile for them and all their descendants after them. Living in exile means living in a perpetual state of disconnection and separation that ultimately leads to death if not remedied. There are four aspects to exile: spiritual, emotional, relational, and physical.

The promise of redemption from exile is also connected to the number four. At the Passover Seder, there are four cups of wine that correspond to the four aspects of redemption mentioned in Exodus 6:6–7 (TLV): "I will bring you out," "I will deliver you," "I will redeem you," "I will take you to Myself." At the final redemption, the Lord will "lift up a banner for the nations, and assemble the dispersed of Israel, and gather the scattered of Judah from the four corners of the earth" (Isaiah 11:12 TLV). . . .

The bleeding woman had been living in exile on all four levels. She had no physical contact with family and friends, could not publicly worship in the temple, was isolated and alone, and lived in a perpetual state of physical pain. But she found a fourfold healing by touching one of the four corners of Jesus' garment, and thus she became an example of the messianic redemption that we can begin to experience right now when we reach out and touch Him! Like her, we must have the faith to boldly reach out and seize the Lord so that we might find help and healing in our time of need.[24]

—From *The Rock, the Road, and the Rabbi*

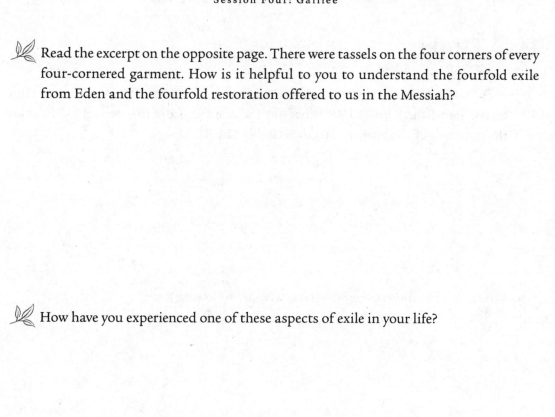

Read the excerpt on the opposite page. There were tassels on the four corners of every four-cornered garment. How is it helpful to you to understand the fourfold exile from Eden and the fourfold restoration offered to us in the Messiah?

How have you experienced one of these aspects of exile in your life?

How has Jesus restored you from that particular aspect of exile?

Day Three

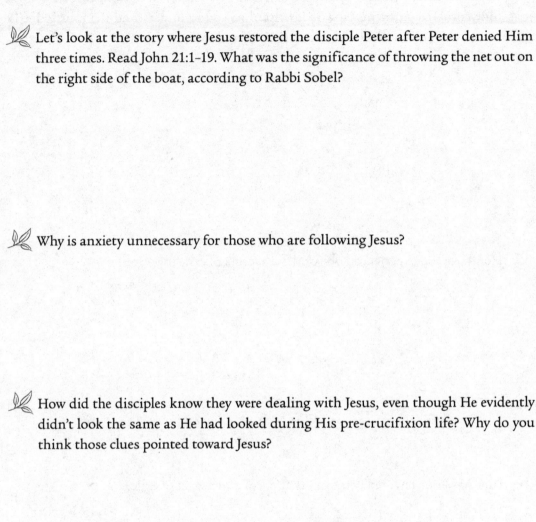

Let's look at the story where Jesus restored the disciple Peter after Peter denied Him three times. Read John 21:1–19. What was the significance of throwing the net out on the right side of the boat, according to Rabbi Sobel?

Why is anxiety unnecessary for those who are following Jesus?

How did the disciples know they were dealing with Jesus, even though He evidently didn't look the same as He had looked during His pre-crucifixion life? Why do you think those clues pointed toward Jesus?

Why did Jesus ask Peter three times if he loved Him?

Do you love Jesus enough to risk losing everything for Him? What evidence of this is there in your life?

About thirty years after this scene with Jesus, Peter was crucified for proclaiming Jesus as Messiah. What risk is God asking you to take for Jesus' sake?

What is the most important thing that you will take away from this session?

REFLECT

Reflect on these points as you close out this week's personal study.

- What "boat" does Jesus want you to get into today? Where does He want you to set sail? Whom does He want you to greet in love and mercy—even if they run away screaming in chaos?

- Consider what you think is spiritually useful about a focus on purity and the connection it might have to restoration in Christ.

- Reflect on how close Peter was to Jesus and yet how easily he denied Him. Think about how Peter's example is relevant in your life and how you might change it.

MOUNT OF OLIVES

The Triumphal Entry

*As they approached Jerusalem and came to Bethphage and Bethany at
the Mount of Olives, Jesus sent two of his disciples, saying to them,
"Go to the village ahead of you, and just as you enter it, you will find
a colt tied there." . . . When they brought the colt to Jesus and threw
their cloaks over it, he sat on it. Many people spread their cloaks on
the road, while others spread branches they had cut in the fields. Those
who went ahead and those who followed shouted, "Hosanna!"
"Blessed is he who comes in the name of the Lord!"*

MARK 11:1—2, 7—9

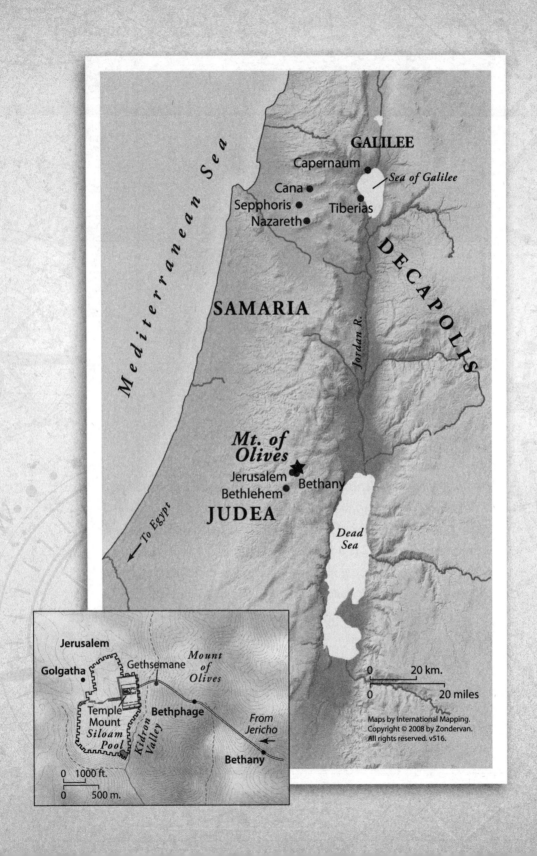

GALILEE

Capernaum

Cana

Sepphoris

Nazareth

Tiberias

Sea of Galilee

DECAPOLIS

Mediterranean Sea

SAMARIA

Jordan R.

Mt. of Olives

Jerusalem

Bethlehem

Bethany

JUDEA

To Egypt

Dead Sea

0   20 km.

0   20 miles

Jerusalem

Golgatha

Gethsemane

Mount of Olives

Temple Mount

Siloam Pool

Kidron Valley

Bethphage

From Jericho

Bethany

0   1000 ft.

0   500 m.

TODAY'S TOUR STOP

Ask someone in the group to read aloud this introduction to today's setting: the Mount of Olives.

The Mount of Olives is actually a two-mile ridge with three summits along it. In Jesus' day, it was covered with olive groves and small villages, such as Bethany and Bethphage. Bethany was situated on a well-traveled road to Jericho. It was the village where Jesus' friends Mary, Martha, and Lazarus lived. Jesus stayed with them on the night before He rode triumphantly into Jerusalem, a few days before His death.

The road from Bethany runs steeply downhill to the Kidron Valley and then up again into Jerusalem's Old City (the city of Jesus' day, which is much smaller than the whole of modern Jerusalem). When Jesus rode a donkey colt down that road less than a week before Passover, there must have been many people in the crowd who expected Him to ride into the temple precincts, take hold of the horns on the altar, and declare Himself to be the Messiah who would drive out the Roman oppressors.

Instead, Jesus entered the temple precincts and drove out the people selling animals for sacrifice, effectively bringing the system of animal sacrifice to a halt for a day. He thereby declared that He was going to replace the animal sacrifices with something better. In this session, we will look at two things that Jesus did on the Mount of Olives: the triumphal ride into Jerusalem and His final night spent in an olive grove called Gethsemane.

FIRST THOUGHTS

Have each person in the group share an answer to these questions:

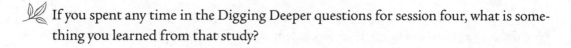 If you spent any time in the Digging Deeper questions for session four, what is something you learned from that study?

If you knew you were going to die within a week, where would you like to spend your last remaining days?

WATCH THE VIDEO

Play the video segment for session five. As you watch, use the outline below to record any thoughts or concepts that stand out to you.

Notes

Jesus didn't come riding on a horse (a symbol of military might) but on a donkey (a symbol of humility), because he was going to humbly surrender his life as a sacrifice.

The Old Testament stories of Abraham's and Moses' use of a donkey points to the fact that Jesus, as the "greater than" of these two men, would bring a greater redemption.

Not only was Jesus' entrance into Jerusalem triumphant, but his return will also be triumphant as he descends and sets foot on the Mount of Olives.

When we pray for the peace of Jerusalem, we are praying for the kingdom of God to come on earth as it is in heaven.

The Garden of Gethsemane means the "place of the olive press," which represents the anguish that Jesus faced on the night of His betrayal.

It is significant that Jesus prayed three times for God to take the cup from Him, for it would take three "pressings" for all the oil to be removed from an olive.

Jesus rode down the Mount of Olives into Jerusalem on a donkey during what has become known as the Triumphal Entry. But did you ever wonder why He chose to ride on a donkey? Every one of Jesus' actions was intentional. He came to fulfill everything that was prophesied by Moses and the prophets concerning the Messiah so that the world might know that He was the promised Redeemer.

Speaking of the coming Messiah, the Old Testament prophet Zechariah wrote:

Rejoice greatly, daughter of Zion!
Shout, daughter of Jerusalem!
Behold, your king is coming to you,
a righteous one bringing salvation.
He is lowly, riding on a donkey—
on a colt, the foal of a donkey (Zechariah 9:9 TLV)

So Jesus the Messiah came riding on a donkey in fulfillment of this prophecy. But there is much more meaning as to why a donkey was chosen. Horses are a symbol of military might, wealth, and strength. Donkeys, on the other hand, are symbolic of humility and peace. At His first coming, Messiah came as the humble lamb of God riding on a donkey. But at His second coming, He will descend from the heavens riding a white war horse ready to vanquish all evil from the world (see Revelation 19:11–16).[25]

—From *The Rock, the Road, and the Rabbi*

DEBRIEFING THE TOUR

Take a few minutes with your group members to discuss what you just watched and explore these concepts in Scripture.

1. What caught your attention most as you viewed the video?

2. Ask for a volunteer to read aloud Luke 19:28–40. According to Rabbi Jason, Jesus rode into Jerusalem on a donkey colt instead of a horse colt (see Matthew 21:7) because "horses are a symbol of military might, wealth, and strength. Donkeys, on the other hand, are symbolic of humility and peace." In what ways are you drawn to the idea of Jesus as the humble lamb of God riding on a donkey?

3. In what ways are you drawn to the idea of Jesus as the warrior riding on a war horse?

4. By riding on a donkey colt into Jerusalem, Jesus was also fulfilling a prophecy in Zechariah 9:9, which reads, "Rejoice greatly, Daughter Zion! Shout, Daughter Jerusalem! See, your king comes to you, righteous and victorious, lowly and riding on a donkey, on a colt, the foal of a donkey." How was the reality of what Jesus did after He rode into Jerusalem different from what His disciples expected?

5. Ask for a volunteer to read aloud Matthew 26:36–46. (Note that Luke 22:39 tells us that Gethsemane was on the Mount of Olives.) How does this scene make the Mount of Olives an important place?

6. How are the events in Gethsemane relevant to your life?

TRYING IT OUT

This is a hands-on activity intended to help you visualize a key scene in the drama of Jesus' life and ministry. You'll need at least one computer or phone, branches or stones, and a magic marker.

Look online for video clips of Jesus riding into Jerusalem on a donkey. How do these clips compare with the way you imagine the scene? What do they add, or not add, to your understanding? Take a branch home with you to remind you of the branches the crowd waved to greet Jesus. (If palms or other suitable branches are not available where you live, take a stone home to represent the stones that would cry out to acclaim Jesus if the crowd were silent.) If you have time, use magic markers to write a significant word on your stone. As you will read in *The Rock, the Road, and the Rabbi*, the stones on the Mount of Olives were the gravestones of the large cemetery that lined the road there.

THAT'S A WRAP

This week, you and your group members looked at the story of Jesus' triumphal ride into Jerusalem and then, in stark contrast, His hour of suffering in Gethsemane. The two events go together. In His ride, Jesus deliberately chose to make a prominent entrance into Jerusalem, drawing many people to acclaim Him as the Messiah, while He avoided declaring Himself to be the Messiah and starting a war with Rome. This state of affairs provoked the chief priests in Jerusalem to conspire to have Him arrested, and the agony in Gethsemane was His response. As you prepare for personal study time this week, think about these events driving toward Jesus' self-sacrifice. Reflect on what these scenes reveal about the kind of king that Jesus was determined to be.

After celebrating Passover, Jesus and His disciples walked to the Mount of Olives, to the Garden of Gethsemane (see Matthew 26:36). The fact that Jesus spent the final hours before His arrest in a garden is significant. First, the fall of man occurred in a garden—so Jesus, who is the second Adam, also entered into a garden as He prepared to give His life to atone for the sin of the first man and woman.

Second, one of the primary titles ascribed to Jesus is "Christ." Growing up, I thought this was His last name. Instead, Christ is the Greek equivalent of the Hebrew word *Mashiach* (Messiah), which means "the Anointed One." Why is this so significant? In ancient Israel, kings were anointed with olive oil as a sign of being chosen and empowered by God to rule. Thus, the term *Messiah* in Judaism came to refer to the promised messianic King and Redeemer who would be anointed with olive oil and, more importantly, by the Spirit of the Lord to establish the kingdom of God.

According to Isaiah, it is out of an olive stump that "a shoot will come forth out of the stem of Jesse, and a branch will bear fruit out of His roots," and "the *Ruach of ADONAI* [Spirit of the Lord] will rest upon Him" as the anointed Messiah from the line of David (Isaiah 11:1–2 TLV). It's amazing to think that Jesus spent one of the most important moments of His life in an olive garden, which is the very type of tree that was most symbolic of His role as Messiah (see Jeremiah 33:15; Zechariah 3:8; 6:12).[26]

—From *The Rock, the Road, and the Rabbi*

CLOSING PRAYER

Lord Jesus, You rode into Jerusalem as a king of peace. You deliberately took actions that would provoke the authorities in Jerusalem to have You arrested. You knew what You were doing, and You walked open-eyed into suffering. You were brave and determined, yet at the same time You were fully human and experienced all of the fear any mortal would feel at taking on the weight of human sin and dying a slow and agonizing death. Enable us to taste Your courage as we face our own lives. Thank You for never forsaking us in our Gethsemanes. In Your royal name we pray, Amen.

RECOMMENDED READING

Read chapters 18 and 21 of *The Rock, the Road, and the Rabbi.*

DIGGING DEEPER

In this session, you traveled to the Mount of Olives, a two-mile ridge outside of Jerusalem covered with olive groves and small villiages, including Bethany. It was on the road from Bethany into Jerusalem that Jesus rode a donkey colt in what we call the "Triumphal Entry," and in was in the Garden of Gethsemane that Jesus, on the night of His arrest, prayed, "My Father, if it is possible, may this cup be taken from me. Yet not as I will, but as you will" (Matthew 26:39). This personal study section will offer you additional Bible passages to dig into on your own to enrich your study of this session's themes. Explore them all or select those that appeal to you.

The donkey plays a key role in the history of the redemption of God's people. We see this in the life of Abraham, the father of the Christian faith. Abraham in Hebraic thought went through ten tests. The final test was the offering of Isaac upon the altar as a sacrifice to the Lord, which demonstrated his great faith (see Hebrews 11). But it was also meant to paint a portrait of God the Father's willingness to offer His Only Son on our behalf. In Genesis 22, Abraham put his supplies on a donkey when he went on the three-day journey to offer Isaac, who was a type (or symbolic figure) of Messiah, as a burnt offering on Mount Moriah (see verse 3).

Moses also made use of a donkey when he was sent by God to redeem the children of Israel from Egypt. In Exodus 4:20, Moses put his wife and children on a donkey. Abraham's and Moses's use of a donkey was ultimately meant to point to the Messiah who would also use a donkey when He came to usher in the start of the messianic kingdom that would come through His sufferings.

Jesus' riding on a donkey not only underscored His humility but also pointed to the fact that He was the greater Abraham. As Jesus said, "Abraham rejoiced to see My day; he saw it and was thrilled" (John 8:56 TLV). Jesus was also the greater prophet like Moses, who came to bring about an even greater redemption (Acts 3:22). Thus the work of redemption that began with Abraham and was taken to the next level by Moses was advanced further by Jesus, who at His Second Coming will bring complete transformation to all of creation.

—From *The Rock, the Road, and the Rabbi*

DAY ONE

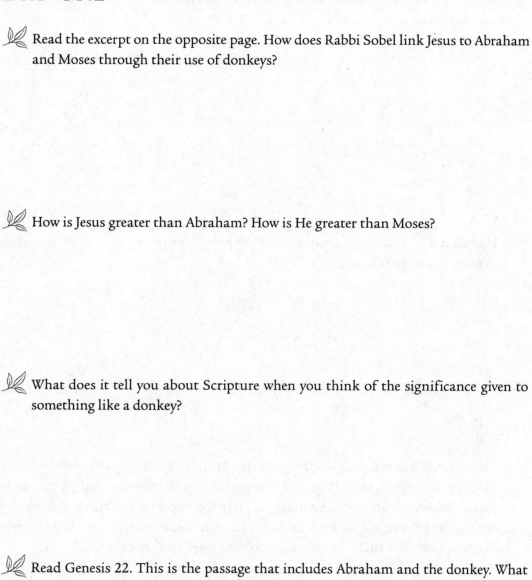

🌿 Read the excerpt on the opposite page. How does Rabbi Sobel link Jesus to Abraham and Moses through their use of donkeys?

🌿 How is Jesus greater than Abraham? How is He greater than Moses?

🌿 What does it tell you about Scripture when you think of the significance given to something like a donkey?

🌿 Read Genesis 22. This is the passage that includes Abraham and the donkey. What role does the donkey play in this story? What do you imagine it was carrying?

🌿 Does it surprise you that the donkey's role is relatively small? Why did you answer the way you did?

🌿 How does this story of Abraham and his son point forward to the story of Jesus? List as many parallels as you can.

🌿 We think of Isaac as a child when we read this story, but according to Jewish tradition, he was in his thirties at this time.[27] Whatever his age might have actually been, we do know that he was at least old enough to carry the wood for the burnt offering (see verse 6), which a child could not have carried. (Enough wood for a small bonfire was needed.) How does this affect the way you view Isaac's role in this story?

DAY TWO

 The mountain in the region of Moriah (see Genesis 22:2) was the same mountain on which King David later chose to build the temple. Read 1 Chronicles 21:16–22:1. This story begins during a plague the Lord sent on Israel because David, in order to feed his pride, had disobeyed the Lord and ordered his soldiers to be counted. How did David learn that the threshing floor mentioned in this passage was going to be the right place to build the temple for the Lord?

 How would you describe the development of David's emotional or mental state from the beginning to the end of this story?

Threshing involved separating wheat from the chaff that encased it. The wheat was then tossed into the air with something a bit like a leaf rake, and the lighter chaff blew away. The threshing floor of Araunah was a high and flat place where there was plenty of wind to blow away the chaff and let the threshed wheat fall to the ground. It was also a good site for a temple that would dominate the skyline.

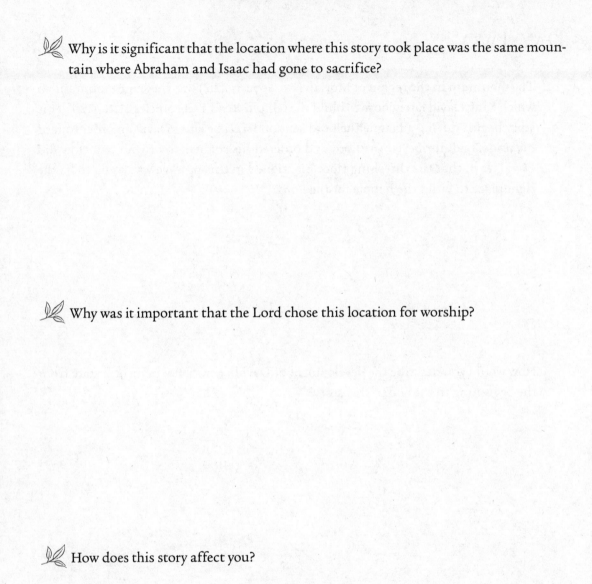

Why is it significant that the location where this story took place was the same mountain where Abraham and Isaac had gone to sacrifice?

Why was it important that the Lord chose this location for worship?

How does this story affect you?

DAY THREE

During your group study, you read about Jesus' triumphal entry in Luke 19:28–40. The following passage in Luke 19:41–44 goes on with the story of what happened when Jesus was approaching Jerusalem on the donkey:

> As he [Jesus] approached Jerusalem and saw the city, he wept over it and said, "If you, even you, had only known on this day what would bring you peace—but now it is hidden from your eyes. The days will come upon you when your enemies will build an embankment against you and encircle you and hem you in on every side. They will dash you to the ground, you and the children within your walls. They will not leave one stone on another, because you did not recognize the time of God's coming to you."

This passage was fulfilled forty years later when the Jews revolted against Rome and the Roman army laid siege to Jerusalem. They eventually burned the city and dismantled the temple stone by stone.

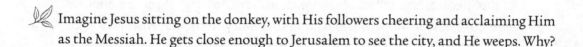 Imagine Jesus sitting on the donkey, with His followers cheering and acclaiming Him as the Messiah. He gets close enough to Jerusalem to see the city, and He weeps. Why?

What does Jesus speak of that would have brought peace to Jerusalem (see verse 42)?

In April AD 70, the Romans laid siege to the city of Jerusalem. Four years earlier, in AD 66, the Jewish people had revolted in response to the harsh policies enacted by the Roman emperor Nero, sparking the start of the First Jewish-Roman War. The siege was led by a general named Titus, who would later become a Roman emperor himself, and it lasted five months.

It took the Roman army only three weeks to break through the first two walls of the city, but then they were met with a stubborn Jewish resistance that halted their advance and kept them from breaking through the third wall. The resistance lasted until August of AD 70, when the Romans finally overwhelmed the defenders and set fire to the temple. The destruction of Jerusalem and the temple marked a turning point in Jewish history.[28]

Jesus had prophesied that enemies would encircle Jerusalem, dash it to the ground, and kill its inhabitants, leaving not one stone on another (see Luke 19:43–44). Josephus, a first-century Roman-Jewish historian, would later describe how these events transpired: "While the holy house [the temple] was on fire, everything was plundered that came to hand, and ten thousand of those that were caught were slain; nor was there a commiseration of any age . . . but children and old men . . . and priests, were all slain in the same manner. . . The flame was also carried a long way, and made an echo, together with the groans of those who were slain . . . one would have thought the whole city would have been on fire. Nor can one imagine anything greater and more terrible than this noise."[29]

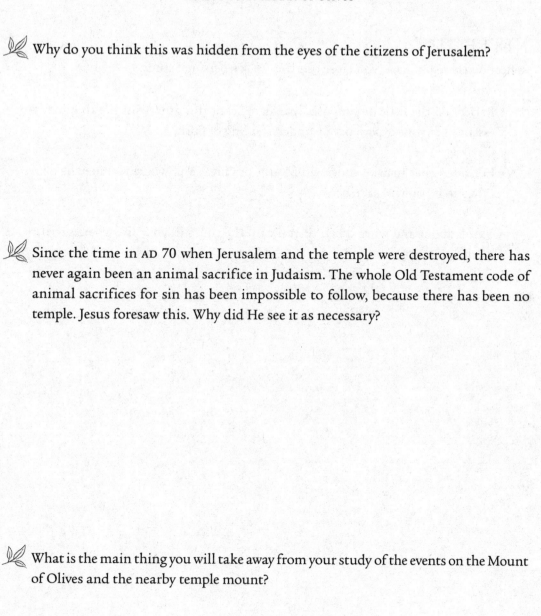

Why do you think this was hidden from the eyes of the citizens of Jerusalem?

Since the time in AD 70 when Jerusalem and the temple were destroyed, there has never again been an animal sacrifice in Judaism. The whole Old Testament code of animal sacrifices for sin has been impossible to follow, because there has been no temple. Jesus foresaw this. Why did He see it as necessary?

What is the main thing you will take away from your study of the events on the Mount of Olives and the nearby temple mount?

REFLECT

Reflect on these points as you close out this week's personal study.

- Reflect on the little or supposedly insignificant things in your life that may be essential to your experience or understanding of faith.

- Consider what may be your own Mount of Olives and where you may be being called to lay down a sacrifice.

- Think about and write down (if you can) the times in your life where sacrifice has led to peace.

JERUSALEM

Crucifixion and Resurrection

Finally Pilate handed him over to them to be crucified.
So the soldiers took charge of Jesus. Carrying his own cross,
he went out to the place of the Skull (which in Aramaic
is called Golgotha). There they crucified him, and with him
two others—one on each side and Jesus in the middle. . . .
Jesus said, "It is finished." With that, he bowed his
head and gave up his spirit.

JOHN 19:16—18, 30

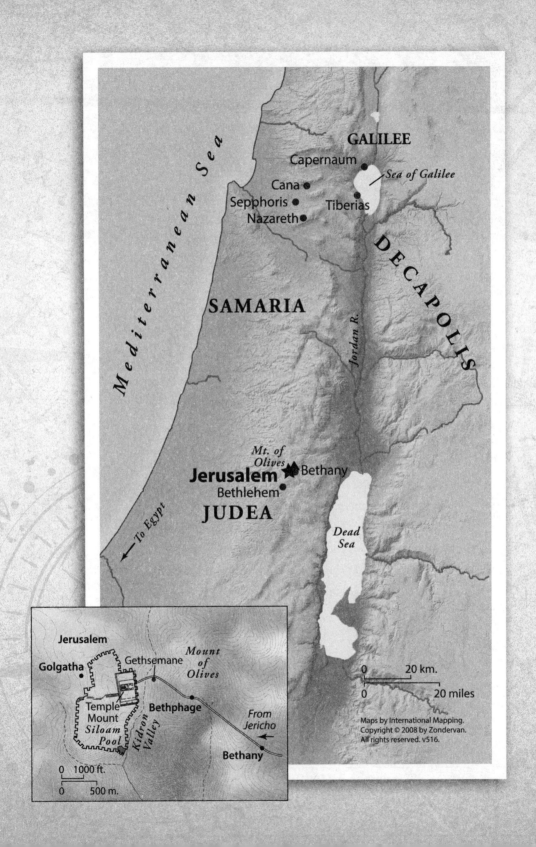

GALILEE

Capernaum

Sea of Galilee

Cana

Sepphoris

Nazareth

Tiberias

Mediterranean Sea

DECAPOLIS

SAMARIA

Jordan R.

Mt. of
Olives

Jerusalem ★ Bethany

Bethlehem

JUDEA

To Egypt

*Dead
Sea*

0   20 km.

0   20 miles

Jerusalem

Golgatha

Gethsemane

*Mount
of
Olives*

Temple
Mount

Bethphage

*Siloam
Pool*

*Kidron
Valley*

*From
Jericho*

Bethany

0   1000 ft.

0   500 m.

TODAY'S TOUR STOP

Ask someone in the group to read aloud this introduction to today's main setting: Jerusalem.

Today, Jerusalem is a large and sprawling city in the modern-day nation of Israel. However, the Old City, the Jerusalem of Jesus' day, covers only about 220 acres—less than a square mile. It was easy to walk across Jerusalem in those days, and even reasonable to walk from Bethany on the Mount of Olives to Jerusalem and back in a day.

The Old City was built on two hilltops at about 2,500 feet above sea level. Valleys and dry riverbeds surrounded it, adding to the defenses once offered by the city wall, which the Roman army demolished during the siege of Jerusalem, four decades after Jesus' death.

Exact figures for the city's population in Jesus' time are impossible, but scholars have estimated between 60,000 and 80,000. When Jesus rode into town on the donkey, we can imagine about 70,000 local citizens and another 70,000 Jews who had come to town for Passover, swelling the city to bursting and adding to the tension in the air. The populace was thirsting for a king to start a war against Rome, and the temple priests and other leaders were doing everything they could to keep a lid on that frenzy.

Many events of Jesus' life took place in Jerusalem. He did a great deal of teaching there. But in this session, we will focus on the most important thing He did there: die. We will look closely at Jesus' journey to the cross and also explore why Jesus had to die on a cross.

FIRST THOUGHTS

Have each person in the group share an answer to these questions:

 If you spent any time in the Digging Deeper questions for session five, what is something you learned from that study?

 What is one thing you are thankful for that you have received from this study of the places where Jesus lived and ministered?

WATCH THE VIDEO

Play the video segment for session six. As you watch, use the outline below to record any thoughts or concepts that stand out to you.

Notes

The crucifixion of Jesus closely follows what was known as a Roman triumph.

The first Adam, through the tree, brought death into the world; but the second Adam brought about a redemption and restoration by means of dying on a tree.

Jesus, through the crown of thorns, took on Himself the curse of creation in order to reverse it and restore the original blessing.

Jesus wasn't just making atonement for Adam but for Eve as well—and all of us.

Just as the first sin took place in a garden, so the atonement for that sin would take place in a garden, when Jesus was placed in a tomb there owned by Joseph of Arimathea.

Jesus rose from the dead on the Feast of the Firstfruits—a good firstfruits was the sign of a greater harvest to come.

The greatest demonstration of God's lovingkindness was the fact that He gave His life for us and rose again on the third day . . . the tomb is empty!

The Bible tells us that Jesus was born during the reign of the Roman emperor Caesar Augustus, [who] vowed to build a temple to honor his murdered father and to hold a dedication ceremony to proclaim his father as divine. During that ceremony, a comet streaked through the sky—a sign that Augustus declared as confirmation that he himself must be "the Son of God," if his father, Julius Caesar, was God. From that period on, the Roman people believed Caesar Augustus to be the divine "Son of God."

What began as a way to honor conquering generals soon became limited to the emperors, proclaiming their sovereignty and divinity. The ceremony began with the Roman soldiers who assembled at the Praetorium, where the guards were stationed. Then a purple robe (the color of royalty) would be placed on the emperor and a wreath would be placed on his head. "Hail Caesar!" they would shout, and the people would chant, "Triomphe!" as the emperor and the guards wound their way along the Via Sacra in Rome to arrive at the Capitoline, or "head hill." There, a bull would be sacrificed by someone who had been carrying an instrument of death.

The emperor would then be offered a bowl of wine, which he would refuse or sometimes pour out on the head of the sacrificial bull. Finally, the emperor would ascend the steps of the Capitoline, accompanied by someone on his left and someone on his right. The entire population would declare him as their "savior"—their divine Caesar, proclaiming, "Hail Caesar, Lord and God!" . . . The description of Jesus' last days in Mark's Gospel perfectly paralleled this Roman procession known as a triumph.[30]

—From *The Rock, the Road, and the Rabbi*

DEBRIEFING THE TOUR

Take a few minutes with your group members to discuss what you just watched and explore these concepts in Scripture.

1. What caught your attention most as you viewed the video?

2. Ask for a volunteer to read aloud Mark 15:6–39. This is the passage from Mark's Gospel that Kathie spoke about—the one that parallels the Roman procession known as the triumph. The festival referred to in verse 6 is Passover. Pilate is the Roman governor, who alone had the legal authority to execute a criminal. So, the chief priests of the temple had handed Jesus over to the governor, rather than killing Him themselves. Why do you think Mark makes such a point of mentioning what Pilate calls Jesus? What is Mark's purpose (which isn't the same as Pilate's purpose)?

3. What does Mark want us to remember about Jesus when we read these details of His last hours? Why is it so important for us to remember this?

4. According to Rabbi Sobel, why did Jesus have to die on a cross?

5. To what in the Old Testament did the crown of thorns point back?

6. What difference does it make to you personally that Jesus is the king of the Jews and the Son of God? How does it affect your life if Jesus is King?

TRYING IT OUT

This is a hands-on activity to help you fix in your mind what you've learned in this session about the truth that Jesus is your King. For this activity, you will need a smartphone, laptop, or computer.

As a group, do an internet search of images of Jesus as King. Consider these questions:

- Which images are meaningful to you? Why?
- Which ones don't you like, and why?
- If you were going to create your own image to remind you that Jesus is your King, what would you include?
- What would you not include? Why?

Now do a search for images of Jesus as *Jewish* King. Think about these questions:

- How are these images similar?
- How are they different?
- Which of them are meaningful to you, and why?

Some Christians don't believe we should use images of Jesus in our devotional life, because one of the Ten Commandments says:

You shall not make for yourself an image in the form of anything in heaven above or on the earth beneath or in the waters below. You shall not bow down to them or worship them; for I, the LORD your God, am a jealous God, punishing the children for the sin of the parents to the third and fourth generation of those who hate me, but showing love to a thousand generations of those who love me and keep my commandments (Exodus 20:4–6).

Other Christians cite Colossians 1:15: "The Son is the image of the invisible God, the firstborn over all creation." However, based on this verse and the fact that Jesus is God come in the flesh and continues to have a body even now that He has returned to the Father, some Christians believe that He has made it legitimate for Christians to use physical images of Him as long as they don't worship them. Thus, movies about the life of Jesus, for example, are legitimate even though movies are images.

What do you think? What role, if any, can images of Jesus play in your life?

If it is preached that Christ has been raised from the dead, how can some of you say that there is no resurrection of the dead? If there is no resurrection of the dead, then not even Christ has been raised. And if Christ has not been raised, our preaching is useless and so is your faith. More than that, we are then found to be false witnesses about God, for we have testified about God that he raised Christ from the dead. . . . And if Christ has not been raised, your faith is futile; you are still in your sins. Then those also who have fallen asleep in Christ are lost. If only for this life we have hope in Christ, we are of all people most to be pitied.

But Christ has indeed been raised from the dead, the firstfruits of those who have fallen asleep. For since death came through a man, the resurrection of the dead comes also through a man. For as in Adam all die, so in Christ all will be made alive. But each in turn: Christ, the firstfruits; then, when he comes, those who belong to him. Then the end will come, when he hands over the kingdom to God the Father after he has destroyed all dominion, authority and power. For he must reign until he has put all his enemies under his feet. The last enemy to be destroyed is death. For he "has put everything under his feet." . . . When he has done this, then the Son himself will be made subject to him who put everything under him, so that God may be all in all (1 Corinthians 15:12–15, 17–28).

THAT'S A WRAP

This week, you and your group members looked at Jesus' journey to the cross and His death on that cross. You were also introduced to the meaning in many of the details of exactly what happened. As you prepare for personal study time this week, think about those details and praise God for being present in the smallest details of life, giving meaning to all of it.

CLOSING PRAYER

Lord Jesus, You gave up Your life so that we could live. You are the king of the Jews, the emperor of the universe. Give us the courage and unselfishness to follow You in the way of the cross, knowing it to be none other than the way of life and peace. We pray in Your great name, Amen.

RECOMMENDED READING

Read chapter 22 of *The Rock, the Road, and the Rabbi.*

DIGGING DEEPER

In this final session, you ended your tour of the Holy Land with a journey to the city of Jerusalem. This was a place that Jesus often visited during His time on earth—He certainly did a lot of teaching there. But in this session, you focused on the *most* important thing that Jesus did there: suffered and died for our sins. This personal study section will offer you additional Bible passages to dig into on your own as you look more closely at Jesus' journey to the cross and why He had to die on a cross. Explore them all or select those that appeal to you.

DAY ONE

Rabbi Sobel explained why Jesus had to die on a cross. He linked back to the story of Adam and Eve. Read the following passages from Genesis 2–3:

Now the LORD God had planted a garden in the east, in Eden; and there he put the man he had formed. The LORD God made all kinds of trees grow out of the ground—trees that were pleasing to the eye and good for food. In the middle of the garden were the tree of life and the tree of the knowledge of good and evil. . . .

The LORD God took the man and put him in the Garden of Eden to work it and take care of it. And the LORD God commanded the man, "You are free to eat from any tree in the garden; but you must not eat from the tree of the knowledge of good and evil, for when you eat from it you will certainly die."

The LORD God said, "It is not good for the man to be alone. I will make a helper suitable for him." . . .

But for Adam no suitable helper was found. So the LORD God caused the man to fall into a deep sleep; and while he was sleeping, he took one of the man's ribs and then closed up the place with flesh. Then the LORD God made a woman from the rib he had taken out of the man, and he brought her to the man.

The man said,

"This is now bone of my bones
　　and flesh of my flesh;
she shall be called 'woman,'
　　for she was taken out of man" (Genesis 2:8–9, 15–18, 20–23).

Now the serpent was more crafty than any of the wild animals the LORD God had made. He said to the woman, "Did God really say, 'You must not eat from any tree in the garden'?"

The woman said to the serpent, "We may eat fruit from the trees in the garden, but God did say, 'You must not eat fruit from the tree that is in the middle of the garden, and you must not touch it, or you will die.'"

"You will not certainly die," the serpent said to the woman. "For God knows that when you eat from it your eyes will be opened, and you will be like God, knowing good and evil."

When the woman saw that the fruit of the tree was good for food and pleasing to the eye, and also desirable for gaining wisdom, she took some and ate it. She also gave some to her husband, who was with her, and he ate it. Then the eyes of both of them were opened, and they realized they were naked; so they sewed fig leaves together and made coverings for themselves.

Then the man and his wife heard the sound of the Lord God as he was walking in the garden in the cool of the day, and they hid from the Lord God among the trees of the garden. But the Lord God called to the man, "Where are you?"

He answered, "I heard you in the garden, and I was afraid because I was naked; so I hid."

And he said, "Who told you that you were naked? Have you eaten from the tree that I commanded you not to eat from?"

The man said, "The woman you put here with me—she gave me some fruit from the tree, and I ate it."

Then the Lord God said to the woman, "What is this you have done?"

The woman said, "The serpent deceived me, and I ate."

So the Lord God said to the serpent, "Because you have done this,

"Cursed are you above all livestock
    and all wild animals!
You will crawl on your belly
    and you will eat dust
    all the days of your life.
And I will put enmity
    between you and the woman
    and between your offspring and hers;
he will crush your head,
    and you will strike his heel."

To the woman he said,

"I will make your pains in childbearing very severe;
    with painful labor you will give birth to children.
Your desire will be for your husband,
    and he will rule over you."

To Adam he said, "Because you listened to your wife and ate fruit from the tree about which I commanded you, 'You must not eat from it,'

> "Cursed is the ground because of you;
>> through painful toil you will eat food from it
>> all the days of your life.
> It will produce thorns and thistles for you,
>> and you will eat the plants of the field.
> By the sweat of your brow
>> you will eat your food
> until you return to the ground,
>> since from it you were taken;
> for dust you are
>> and to dust you will return."

Adam named his wife Eve, because she would become the mother of all the living.

The Lord God made garments of skin for Adam and his wife and clothed them. And the Lord God said, "The man has now become like one of us, knowing good and evil. He must not be allowed to reach out his hand and take also from the tree of life and eat, and live forever." So the Lord God banished him from the Garden of Eden to work the ground from which he had been taken. After he drove the man out, he placed on the east side of the Garden of Eden cherubim and a flaming sword flashing back and forth to guard the way to the tree of life (Genesis 3:1–24).

 What role do trees play in these two passages from Genesis?

How is the cross like a tree?

What does it say about God that He wanted to redeem humans with a tree?

What does this say about the way He thinks?

Rabbi Sobel calls Jesus "the second Adam." In what ways is Jesus a second Adam? Think about what Adam was called to be and how Jesus fulfilled that.

As always, there is even more. As Jesus hung on the cross, He had a crown of thorns on His head. Have you ever wondered why? The Roman soldiers put a crown of thorns on His head to mock His claim to be King Messiah. But the deeper spiritual reason for the crown of thorns also ties back to the garden of Eden. The sign of the curse of creation was that the ground would "produce thorns and thistles" (Genesis 3:18). By wearing a crown of thorns at His crucifixion, Jesus, the second Adam, took upon Himself the curse of creation, to undo it for the purpose of restoring the blessing!

Not only was Jesus' head pierced, but His hands, feet, and side were pierced as well. His hands were pierced, for it was with human hands that Adam and Eve stole from the tree. His side was pierced, because it was Eve, the one taken from Adam's side, who led Adam into temptation— I believe that by having His side pierced, Jesus was making atonement for the woman's role in the fall.

Finally, Jesus' feet were pierced, because the first messianic prophecy states that the seed of the woman, meaning the messianic seed, would come and crush the head of the serpent, as stated in Genesis 3:14–15. . . . Messiah's hands and feet were pierced so that He might overcome sin, Satan, and death for our sake. And Jesus wearing the crown of thorns demonstrates that He loved us so much that He was willing to identify with our pain and suffering and taste death so that we might experience life![31]

—From *The Rock, the Road, and the Rabbi*

Day Two

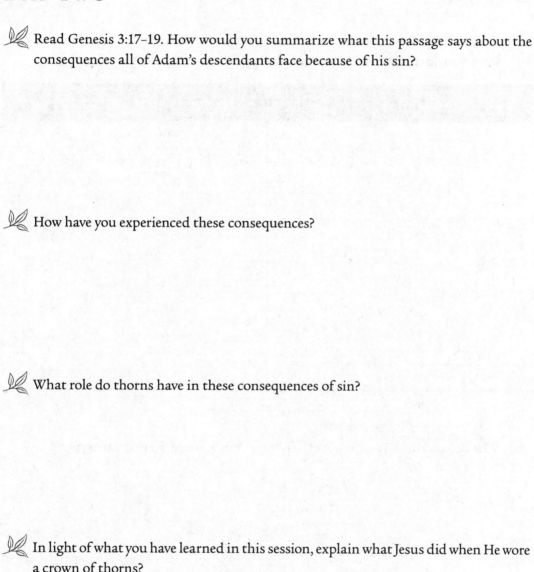 Read Genesis 3:17–19. How would you summarize what this passage says about the consequences all of Adam's descendants face because of his sin?

How have you experienced these consequences?

What role do thorns have in these consequences of sin?

In light of what you have learned in this session, explain what Jesus did when He wore a crown of thorns?

Day Three

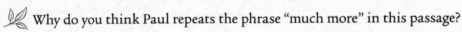 Read Romans 5:1–19. In the chart below, show what resulted from Adam's actions and from Jesus' actions.

Through Adam	Through Christ

 Why do you think Paul repeats the phrase "much more" in this passage?

 How is what Jesus did much more than what Adam did?

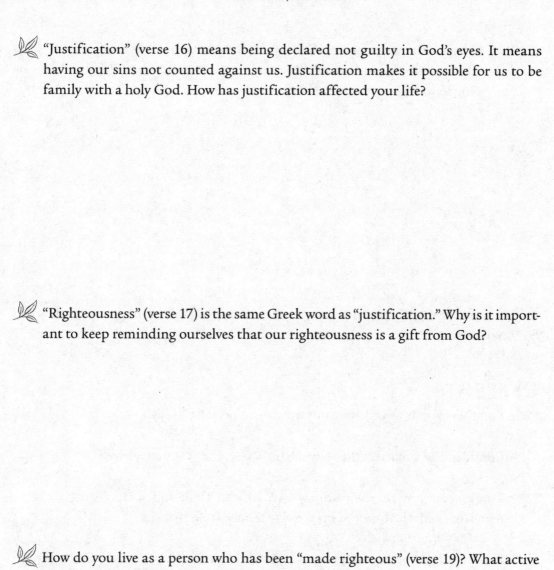

"Justification" (verse 16) means being declared not guilty in God's eyes. It means having our sins not counted against us. Justification makes it possible for us to be family with a holy God. How has justification affected your life?

"Righteousness" (verse 17) is the same Greek word as "justification." Why is it important to keep reminding ourselves that our righteousness is a gift from God?

How do you live as a person who has been "made righteous" (verse 19)? What active things do you do because you have been made righteous?

List at least three key insights that you have gained from this study of the places where Jesus lived and ministered. What are the most important takeaways that you are going to weave into your life?

Tell someone one of these insights. Send a message to a friend, or post your thoughts on social media.

REFLECT
Reflect on these points as you close out this week's personal study.

- Consider why it matters that Jesus' hands, feet, and side were pierced.

- Think about any thorns you may have in your flesh and what sin they may represent—and whether or not you feel redeemed from that sin.

- Reflect on how you live as a person who has been declared not guilty in God's eyes, despite your tendency to sin.

- Make it a point in your daily life to remember Jesus is King. Focus on Him rather than what hinders you. Claim His reign in your life.

LEADER'S GUIDE

Thank you for your willingness to lead your group through this study! What you have chosen to do is valuable and will make a great difference in the lives of others. *The Rock, the Road, and the Rabbi* is a six-session Bible study built around video content and small-group interaction. As the group leader, imagine yourself as the host of a party. Your job is to take care of your guests by managing the details so that when your guests arrive, they can focus on one another and on the interaction around the topic for that session.

Your role as the group leader is not to answer all the questions or reteach the content—the video, book, and study guide will do most of that work. Your job is to guide the experience and cultivate your small group into a connected and engaged community. This will make it a place for members to process, question, and reflect—not necessarily receive more instruction.

There are several elements in this leader's guide that will help you as you structure your study and reflection time, so be sure to follow along and take advantage of each one.

BEFORE YOU BEGIN

Before your first meeting, make sure the group members have a copy of this study guide. Alternatively, you can hand out the study guides at your first meeting and give the members some time to look over the material and ask any preliminary questions. Also make sure they are aware that they have access to the streaming videos at any time by following the instructions provided. During your first meeting, ask the members to provide their name, phone number, and email address so you can keep in touch with them.

Generally, the ideal size for a group is eight to ten people, which will ensure that everyone has enough time to participate in discussions. If you have more people, you might want to break up the main group into smaller subgroups. Encourage those who show up at the first meeting to commit to attending the duration of the study, as this will help the group members get to know one another, create stability for the group, and help you know how to best prepare to lead them through the material.

Each of the sessions begins with an opening reflection called "Today's Tour Stop." The questions that follow in the "First Thoughts" section serve as a sort of icebreaker to get the group members thinking about the topic. Some people may want to tell a long story in response to one of these questions, but the goal is to keep the answers brief. Ideally, you want everyone in the group to get a chance to answer, so try to keep the responses to a minute or less. If you have talkative group members, say up front that everyone needs to limit their answer to one minute.

Give the group members a chance to answer, but tell them to feel free to pass if they wish. With the rest of the study, it's generally not a good idea to have everyone answer every question—a free-flowing discussion is more desirable. But with the opening icebreaker questions, you can go around the circle. Encourage shy people to share, but don't force them.

At your first meeting, let the group members know each session contains a personal study section they can use to continue to engage with the content until the next meeting. While this is optional, it will help them cement the concepts presented during the group study time and help them better understand the life, ministry, and death of Jesus. Let them know that if they choose to do so, they can watch the video for the next session by accessing the streaming code. Invite them to bring any questions and insights to your next meeting, especially if they had a breakthrough moment or didn't understand something.

PREPARATION FOR EACH SESSION

As the leader, there are a few things you should do to prepare for each meeting:

- **Read through the session.** This will help you become more familiar with the content and know how to structure the discussion times.

- **Decide how the videos will be used.** Determine whether you want the members to watch the videos ahead of time (again, via the streaming access code provided with this guide) or together as a group.

- **Decide which questions you want to discuss.** Based on the length of your group discussions, you may not be able to get through all the questions. So look over the questions in each session and choose which ones you definitely want to cover.

- **Be familiar with the questions you want to discuss.** When the group meets, you'll be watching the clock, so make sure you are familiar with the questions that you have selected. In this way, you will ensure that you have the material more deeply in your mind than your group members.

- **Pray for your group.** Pray for your group members and ask God to lead them as they study His Word.

In many cases, there will be no one "right" answer to the question. Answers will vary, especially when the group members are being asked to share their personal experiences.

STRUCTURING THE DISCUSSION TIME

You will need to determine with your group how long you want to meet so you can plan your time accordingly. If you would like to meet for ninety minutes, follow the suggested times for each section in the left-hand column. If you would prefer for your group to meet for two hours each week, follow the times given in the right-hand column.

Section	90 Minutes	120 Minutes
FIRST THOUGHTS (discuss the opening questions for the session)	15 minutes	20 minutes
WATCH THE VIDEO (watch the teaching material together and take notes)	20 minutes	20 minutes
DEBRIEFING THE TOUR (discuss the questions you selected ahead of time)	35 minutes	50 minutes
TRYING IT OUT (do the closing activity given for each session)	10 minutes	15 minutes
CLOSING PRAYER (pray together and dismiss)	10 minutes	15 minutes

It will be up to you to keep things on schedule. You might want to set a timer for each segment so both you and the group members know when your time is up. Don't be concerned if the group members are quiet or slow to share. People are often quiet when they are pulling together their ideas, and this might be a new experience for them. Just ask a question and let it hang in the air until someone shares. You can then say, "Thank you. What about others? What came to you when you watched that portion of the teaching?"

GROUP DYNAMICS

Leading a group through *The Rock, the Road, and the Rabbi* will prove to be highly rewarding both to you and your group members. But you still may encounter challenges along the way! Discussions can get off track. Group members may not be sensitive to the needs and ideas of others. Some might worry they will be expected to talk about matters that make them feel awkward. Others may express comments that result in disagreements. To help ease this strain on you and the group, consider the following ground rules:

- When someone raises a question or comment that is off the main topic, suggest that you deal with it another time, or, if you feel led to go in that direction, let the group know you will be spending some time discussing it.

- If someone asks a question that you don't know how to answer, admit it and move on. At your discretion, feel free to invite group members to comment on questions that call for personal experience.

- If you find one or two people are dominating the discussion time, direct a few questions to others in the group. Outside the main group time, ask the more dominating members to help you draw out the quieter ones. Work to make them a part of the solution instead of part of the problem.

- When a disagreement occurs, encourage the group members to process the matter in love. Encourage those on opposite sides to restate what they heard the other side say about the matter, and then invite each side to evaluate if that perception is accurate. Lead the group in examining other passages of Scripture related to the topic and look for common ground.

When any of these issues arise, encourage your group members to follow these words from Scripture: "Love one another" (John 13:34), "If it is possible, as far as it depends on you, live at peace with everyone" (Romans 12:18), and "Be quick to listen, slow to speak and slow to become angry" (James 1:19). This will make your group time more rewarding and beneficial for everyone who attends.

Thank you again for taking the time to lead your group through *The Rock, the Road, and the Rabbi*. You are making a difference in your group members' lives and having an impact on their journey as they learn more about Jesus, the Messiah.

ABOUT THE AUTHORS

Kathie Lee Gifford, four-time Emmy Award winner, is best known for her eleven years cohosting the popular fourth hour of *TODAY* alongside Hoda Kotb. She has authored numerous books, including her most recent book, *The God of the Way*, and five *New York Times* bestselling books, including *The Rock, the Road, and the Rabbi* and *It's Never Too Late*. She is also an actress, singer, songwriter, playwright, producer, and director.

Rabbi Jason Sobel is the founder of Fusion Global. He received his rabbinic ordination from the UMJC (Union of Messianic Jewish Congregations) in 2005, his B.A. in Jewish Studies at Moody, and his M.A. in Intercultural Studies from Southeastern Seminary. He is the author of *Mysteries of the Messiah, Signs and Secrets of the Messiah,* and is coauthor of the *New York Times* bestseller *The Rock, the Road, and the Rabbi*, with Kathie Lee Gifford.

ENDNOTES

1. R. T. France, "The Gospel of Matthew," *New International Commentary on the New Testament* (Grand Rapids: Eerdmans, 2007).
2. Russell E. Saltzman, "Biblical Travel: How Far to Where, and What About the Donkey?" Aleteia, January 24, 2017, https://aleteia.org/2017/01/24/biblical-travel-how-far-to-where-and-what-about-the-donkey/.
3. "In Luke 2:7 Is 'Kataluma' a 'Guestroom' in a House or at an 'Inn'?" Biblical Hermeneutics, Stack Exchange, https://hermeneutics.stackexchange.com/questions/749/in-luke-27-is-kataluma-a-guestroom-in-a-house-or-at-an-inn.
4. "What Is the Feast of Tabernacles/Booths/Sukkot?" Got Questions, https://www.gotquestions.org/Feast-of-Tabernacles.html.
5. Paul William Roberts, "Secret Lives of the Wise Men," *The New York Times*, December 25, 1995, https://www.nytimes.com/1995/12/25/opinion/secret-lives-of-the-wise-men.html#:~:text=Matthew's%20wise%20men%2C%20or%20Magi,at%20the%20birth%20of%20Christ.
6. Kathie Lee Gifford with Rabbi Jason Sobel, *The Rock, the Road, and the Rabbi* (Nashville, TN: W Publishing, 2018), 120–121.
7. John Dart, "Up Against Caesar," SBL Forum, n.p. (cited April 2005), http://sbl-site.org/Article.aspx?ArticleID=388.
8. E. Meyers and J. Strange, *Archaeology, the Rabbis, and Early Christianity* (Nashville: Abingdon, 1981); "Nazareth" article in the Anchor Bible Dictionary (New York: Doubleday, 1992).
9. "Herod Antipas," Wikipedia.com, https://en.wikipedia.org/wiki/Herod_Antipas.
10. Gifford and Sobel, *The Rock, the Road, and the Rabbi*, 41–43.
11. "Mount Precipice," Wikipedia, https://en.wikipedia.org/wiki/Mount_Precipice.
12. In Hebrew texts of the Bible, Zechariah 1:18–21 is numbered 2:1–4.
13. Talmud, Babylonian Sukkah, 52.
14. Gifford and Sobel, *The Rock, the Road, and the Rabbi*, 43–44.
15. Gifford and Sobel, *The Rock, the Road, and the Rabbi*, 44.
16. Gifford and Sobel, *The Rock, the Road, and the Rabbi*, 59–60.
17. Mark T. Schuler, "Recent Archaeology of Galilee and the "Interpretation of Texts from the Galilean Ministry of Jesus," *Concordia Theological Quarterly*, vol. 71:2, April 2007, 103–104, http://www.ctsfw.net/media/pdfs/schuler recentarchaeology.pdf; Jonathan L. Reed, *Archaeology and the Galilean Jesus: A Reexamination of the Evidence* (Harrisburg, PA: Trinity Press International, 2000), 152.
18. Gifford and Sobel, *The Rock, the Road, and the Rabbi*, 63–65.
19. Gifford and Sobel, *The Rock, the Road, and the Rabbi*, 68–69.
20. D. A. Carson, "Matthew," *The Expositor's Bible Commentary* (Grand Rapids, MI: Zondervan, 2010), 238–239; "Centurion: Roman Military Officer," Brittanica, https://www.britannica.com/topic/centurion-Roman-military-officer.
21. Gifford and Sobel, *The Rock, the Road, and the Rabbi*, 82–83.
22. Gifford and Sobel, *The Rock, the Road, and the Rabbi*, 104–105.
23. Gifford and Sobel, *The Rock, the Road, and the Rabbi*, 85–86.
24. Gifford and Sobel, *The Rock, the Road, and the Rabbi*, 87–88.
25. Gifford and Sobel, *The Rock, the Road, and the Rabbi*, 111.
26. Gifford and Sobel, *The Rock, the Road, and the Rabbi*, 127–128.
27. Kathie Lee Gifford and Rabbi Jason Sobel, *The God of the Way* (Nashville, TN: W Publishing, 2022), 20.
28. "Siege of Jerusalem," Wikipedia, https://en.wikipedia.org/wiki/Siege_of_Jerusalem_(70_CE)#:~:text=The%20Temple%20was%20captured%20and,passion%20alone%20was%20in%20command.
29. Josephus, "Of the War," chapter 5, part 1, in *The Wars of the Jews* (written c. AD 75–79).
30. Gifford and Sobel, *The Rock, the Road, and the Rabbi*, 131–132.
31. Gifford and Sobel, *The Rock, the Road, and the Rabbi*, 138–140.

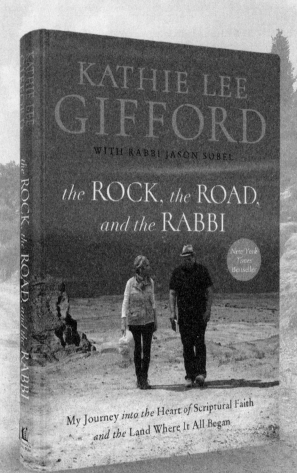